Lori Jakiela's *Portrait of the Artist as a Bingo Worker* is a hilarious, working-class hero of an essay collection. It's full of mall employees, flight attendants, working mothers, struggling writers, loving daughters, and adopted children, who all end up being one person named Lori Jakiela. A book of many masks, it proves the saying: there is no such thing as an ordinary life.
—Scott McClanahan, author of *The Sarah Book*.

OTHER BOOKS BY LORI JAKIELA:

Miss New York Has Everything (Hatchette, 2006)
Spot the Terrorist! (poems—Turning Point, 2011)
The Bridge to Take When Things Get Serious (C&R Press,
    2012; WPA Press, 2015)
Belief Is Its Own Kind of Truth, Maybe (Atticus, 2015)—
    winner of the 2016 William Saroyan Prize for
    International Writing from Stanford University

AUTHOR'S NOTE

This is primarily a work of nonfiction. Situations may have appeared in other works in different forms and different contexts. Characters are not conflated. Events may sometimes be compressed and presented out of sequence. Many names and details have been changed to protect identities. Based on my own memories, the narrative is faithful to my recollections.

BOTTOM DOG PRESS

PORTRAIT OF THE ARTIST AS A BINGO WORKER
ON WORK AND THE WRITING LIFE

LORI JAKIELA

HARMONY MEMOIR SERIES
BOTTOM DOG PRESS
HURON, OHIO

CREDITS:
General Editor: Larry Smith
Cover and Layout Design: Susanna Sharp-Schwacke
Cover Image: "German United Independent Evangelical
Congregation: Bingo" by Chuck Beard
at Abandoned Pittsburgh Gallery
http://abandonedpittsburgh.com

Interior Images by permission of the author

ACKNOWLEDGMENTS
Endless gratitude to the editors of the publications in which the following pieces first appeared:
"Studs," *Pittsburgh Quarterly*; "Portrait of the Artist as a Bingo Worker," *Electric Literature*; "Wonderland of Knowledge," *Defunct*; "Things to Remember," *Purple Clover*; "I'm Into Leather," *KGB BarLit*; "I Felt Like Licking Might Happen a Lot" and "It's Over Before You Know It," *Hobart*; "Rough Air," *Vol. 1 Brooklyn*; "You'll Love the Way We Fly," "Incisions," "Holy," and "There Is No Dust in My House," *Brevity*; "Sexy NYC," *The Rumpus*; "Maybe Nobody's Born Anything" and "Cage Match," *Full Grown People*; "There She Is, Your Ideal," *LitHub*; "The Plain Unmarked Box Arrived," *The New York Times* "Modern Love" column; "Shut Up & Dance," *Belt Magazine*; "Literary Salon," *Mr. Beller's Neighborhood*; "How Will I Use This In, Like, The Real World," *The Pittsburgh Post-Gazette*.

Personal Acknowledgments Continued on Page 213

TABLE OF CONTENTS

The author at age 17, high school senior photo.

Prologue:
Studs

I met the great oral historian and journalist Studs Terkel when I was 18 years old. I didn't know much about Studs back then, only that he was a writer and a pretty famous one, and since I wanted to be a writer too, it was probably a good idea to go see him.

I was a freshman at a college in Erie, Pennsylvania, and deep into my tortured young-writer phase. I wore black velvet culottes. I paired these with knee socks and hair bows and puffy shirts that would have looked great on pirates. I'd quote Jake Barnes from Hemingway's *The Sun Also Rises* ("Isn't it pretty to think so"), and I'd try to drink boilermakers — unsuccessful — and smoke cherry cigars — unsuccessful — and use Wite-Out to smudge the birthdate on my ID so I could hang out in old-man bars.

This was the 1980s, which explains some things and not others.

I hadn't read Joseph Mitchell's *McSorley's Wonderful Saloon*, but I'd read enough Hemingway to believe old-man bars were where I'd find my own lost generation.

I was convinced of this when I met a one-armed man at The Decade in Pittsburgh. He was very drunk. He took a match, lit it off a cigarette, and held it in front of me.

"People," he said, "make matchsticks from the mysteries of trees."

I thought this was a good line, very deep. Maybe it is deep. After all, I remember it many years later and have stolen it here.

Still, I leaned over and blew the match out in one sigh-laden puff.

I tried my best to cultivate snarky world-weariness a la Dorothy Parker back then, but I was prone to giggling, and although I was sharp-tongued, I was two beats slow on the Parker scale. Giggling in velvet culottes makes world-weariness difficult. It makes faking an ID in old-man bars nearly impossible.

Most of the time, I looked a lot like what I was — confused.

I'd grown up in Trafford, a working-class mill town outside of Pittsburgh.

"It's not work," my grandmother Ethel would say, "if it doesn't show in your hands."

My hands were smooth. My boyfriend's mother tried to get me a job as a hand model for the J.C. Penney catalog. My parents had given me privileges they never had. I studied poetry in college. When people asked me what I wanted to be, I was embarrassed to say "writer," so I said "Barbara Walters," which seemed more practical, especially in the years before *The View*.

Studs Terkel, when I first met him, confused me, too. He showed up in his trademark red-checked shirt and red socks. His hair was thick and white and pushed back from his face, which was open and friendly and looked the opposite of world-weary. Studs was always excited about people, their stories, their hearts. He was excited about the world and everything in it. He was not embarrassed of this.

"My birth," he said when he took the podium, "was a momentous occasion. I was born the same day the Titanic sank. The Titanic went down and I came up."

This, I would learn, was the way he always introduced himself. He also always rode the bus because he wanted to be with people and hear their stories. The red-checked shirt was so people would recognize him and talk to him. He loved his wife, Ida, and he loved the sound of the human voice above all things. He had a laugh that shook his whole self out.

His critics would call him sentimental. I, like thousands of other people who would be changed by Studs' work, would call him something else. Human. Humane. Real.

Studs didn't play at being a writer. He was one. He wasn't morose, weighed down by gravitas, black-rimmed glasses and a pretentious scarf. He looked more like my Uncle Tony after a few beers.

My Uncle Tony had been a steelworker and numbers-runner. He used to slip me sips of Iron City beer and terrible homemade wine, and he'd tell me that, if I'd let him pick me up by my ponytail just one time, it would toughen me up for life. My uncle was a story-teller who liked to hear stories back.

Before Studs Terkel, I'd never met a real writer. I didn't expect one to seem so familiar.

"You'll hurt your eyes," my mother would say when she'd catch me reading too much. "You'll get ideas."

Like the ideas I already had about writers and writing.

I hadn't yet read Studs' book, *Working*, though I knew about it. A year earlier, Studs had visited a high school in nearby Girard, PA, where parents and some administrators were leading a movement to ban the book.

In *Working*, Studs lets people talk in their own voices about their own lives. He interviews steelworkers, waitresses, housewives. One chapter features an interview with a hooker, which had the Girard-ians' panties in a twist. Studs said he'd come to Girard to see what made the people there tick. He said he'd come to encourage students to work hard, live honest lives, and read.

A year later, he was back in Erie to do it again.

I went to see Studs at the urging of my writing teacher, a patient man who thought maybe it would do me some good to spend time with Studs, who I would learn was patient and good himself and who wouldn't call me out as the idiot I was.

Most of my early writing years were like this—groping around in darkness, with this book or that book the only light in the mine.

Later, after Studs' reading and talk, after he patted my hand and told me, "You'll be fine. We all will be, you know," after I watched him shuffle out of the auditorium, I read *Working* for the first time.

I grew up with work—my father was a machinist, my mother a nurse, my Uncle Tony and so on. I started waitressing when I was 12. I worked for my grandmother, who, at 230 pounds, ran the kitchen at the Trafford Polish Club with the grace and intensity of a mob boss.

At 18, I believed that, to be a writer, I needed to abandon everyone and everything I knew. I needed to have experiences, a word I'd italicize with my voice and an eye roll. I believed I needed to go to Paris like Hemingway and have my own moveable feast.

No one had yet taught me to write what I knew. Even if they tried, I wouldn't have listened. I believed my life, what I knew, was too ordinary and small to be worthy of art.

But in Studs' work, there were these voices, so familiar to me, voices exactly like the ones I'd listened to

when I was small and could hide under my grandmother's dining room table during Sunday dinners, all
of my aunts' and uncles' legs around me, fences that
held me in and gave me a framework I wouldn't understand for years.

I'd listen to my Aunt Peggy talk about her mammo-
gram—"Don't laugh," she'd say to my Uncle Bus. "You
wouldn't like it if they made grilled cheese out of you."

I'd listen to my mother, the nurse, talk about her
patients—the one who threw his bedpan, the dying one
who saved popsicle sticks from her meal trays and made
them into sculptures, the psych patient who put his
hospital pants on backwards and asked her to dance.

"See?" he said about his pants. "I can't hurt you."

The men in my family didn't talk much. Maybe it
was because they thought no one would be interested
in their stories from the mills, or maybe it was because
their days were so loud with the sounds of metal and
machines they valued quiet, or maybe it was because
work had worn them down and they were too tired to
talk, and so their stories were lost with them.

It's important not to lose those stories. I learned that
from reading *Working*. Everyone's life matters and is
worthy of art. There is no such thing as an ordinary life.

And the most important thing, maybe—don't be a
phony.

I teach college now, so it's important for me to remember that last one. When I was first hired, a professor who'd been at it for decades told me the secret to
surviving academia. "Elevate the diction," she said.
"Never let them see what you don't know."

I thought it was terrible advice and a flat, sad way
to live. I still do, though I understand why people fol-

low it. If people don't understand what you're saying, it's difficult for them to question it.

"I always love to quote Albert Einstein," Studs said, "because nobody dares contradict him."

Every semester now, I teach Studs' work to my students and try not to tear up when I tell them my favorite Studs story. It's about the time he was mugged on the streets of his beloved Chicago. I don't know if the story's true or not, but I believe it. The story goes, the mugger jumps Studs. Studs and the mugger roll around on the ground. The mugger goes for Studs' wallet, but Studs wants to talk.

"So how many of these jobs do you do a day?" he asks the mugger. "How much do you get for a job like this?"

Another thing Studs taught me: World-weariness is for chumps. Stay curious. Know yourself. Be true to yourself.

In *Working*, Studs has a chapter on Mike Lefevre, a steelworker like my father and uncles, who talks about his dream job:

"I'd like to run a combination bookstore and tavern. (Laughs.) I would like to have a place where college kids came and a steelworker could sit down and talk. Where a workingman could not be ashamed of Walt Whitman and where a college professor could not be ashamed that he painted his house over the weekend.

"If a carpenter built a cabin for poets, I think the least the poets owe the carpenter is just three or four one-liners on the wall. A little plaque: 'Though we labor with our minds, this place we can relax in was built by someone who can work with his hands. And his work is as noble as ours.'

"I think the poet owes something to the guy who builds the cabin for him."

I believe that.

I'm 53 years old, a professor and writer.

Sometimes I work weekends as a waitress for a catering company.

I need the money.

I love the job.

PART 1

The author, age 10, with her grandmother Ethel (r) and one of
Ethel's neighbors—decidedly not Fanny.

Portrait of the Artist as a Bingo Worker

I worked bingo nights at the Trafford Polish Club on Mondays and Wednesdays. I was 17 and worked for my grandmother Ethel, who ran the kitchen. Ethel was 230 bad-tempered polka-loving pounds in a housedress and slippers.

"I don't need to impress anybody," Ethel said. "I don't gussy up."

Ethel shouted misery and joy, nothing in between. I'd been working for her since I was 12. None of Ethel's seven other grandchildren would even consider it, such was the abuse, but I prided myself on my endurance. I also liked the money for clothes and books and music.

At 17 I was partial to black velvet culottes and fedoras I'd find at Goodwill. I'd just discovered poetry, classics like Walt Whitman and Emily Dickinson and E. E. Cummings. I spent a lot of money on hardbacks at Walden Books in Monroeville Mall, where I also found Rod McKuen, a 1970s sap poet and songwriter whose critically-bashed books like *Listen to the Warm* and *Caught in the Quiet* matched my angsty teenage heart.

I liked McKuen because he had translated Jacque Brel's "Le Moribund" into "Seasons in the Sun," a song about dying young which I'd play on repeat, *goodbye to you my trusted friend.* I liked that McKuen looked sensitive in his sweaters and berets and that he was adopted, like me. He wrote a memoir called *Finding My Father: One Man's Search for Identity*, a book that critics didn't hate too much and which I snagged from Walden's discount bin and sneak-read in Ethel's Polish Club kitchen.

"You're going to ruin your eyes," Ethel said when she caught me reading.

"Idle hands are devil's playthings," she'd say and hand me a bag of cheeseballs to fry.

*　　　*　　　*

Ethel paid me what she felt like paying, depending, but there were tips and everything was cash, wads of ones that, on a good night, made me feel stripper-rich. I could pocket bills, but a lot of the senior citizens at bingo tipped in change and Ethel made me put the coins in a jar she tallied every night. She called change-tips "found money."

Found money, Ethel claimed, was lucky and meant to be shared. She traded it for instant bingo tickets, the kind where you pull the paper flaps back to see if they spell out "Bingo" or the message "Sorry You Are Not an Instant Winner."

Ethel and I were supposed to split the tickets and winnings 50/50, though I don't remember ever agreeing to that. I think, when Ethel hit, she kept it secret. I'd win a dollar here or there, but never enough to make back what was in the jar.

"You weren't born lucky like me," Ethel said more than once.

"We're family," Ethel said as she doled out my pay from her apron pocket. "And family is more important than money. Family is more important than anything. Remember that."

And so I didn't count my money until I got home, where I closed my bedroom door and spread it out on my bed and sorted it into piles and tried not to do the math when I knew my grandmother shorted me.

"Be grateful," Ethel said. "You kids today are never satisfied."

*   *   *

I wasn't satisfied. Still, most days I worked hard despite it. I was raised to believe in work and family, and I wanted my grandmother to love me even though I was adopted and not family in the sense she meant when she invoked it.

"Your mother couldn't have children of her own, so we got you," Ethel said about my arrival into her family.

Ethel—old-school, first-generation American—believed in blood. I believed I could win her over anyway.

"Who is not a love seeker?" Rod McKuen said, but for adopted people like him and me, people who grew up believing in family as a dotted line, something that at any time could turn null and void and send us back to whatever lost place we'd come from, so much depended upon being loveable.

And so I tried to please my grandmother. I didn't complain much. I tried to look pretty and pleasant. I hid my books under the prep table, and I was okay with the smell of grease and fish and with cleaning up whatever mess Ethel made. I tolerated Ethel's habit of eyeing up my boobs to see if they were growing. I turned when she made me turn left, then right, then left so she could get a good look.

"You been letting boys play with those?" she said until I curled into myself like one of the ingrown toenails I'd clip from Ethel's feet because she couldn't bend down to reach them herself.

Safe sex, Ethel said, meant never letting a boy get on top of you. Safe sex, Ethel said, meant staying away from boys, period.

At 17, I didn't have a steady boyfriend, and the few dates I'd gone on weren't promising. I somehow decided boys found it irresistible when girls went to sleep on them. I am not sure how I decided this—from Rod McKuen lyrics maybe, or romantic movies where the camera zooms in on a beautiful girl sleeping then cuts to a boy who looks on lovingly, tucks a blanket to her chin, and watches her all night long.

Whatever it was, I made a habit of resting my head onto boys' shoulders and pretending to sleep. I learned I could pretend-sleep anywhere. I zonked out on boys at basketball games and school musicals and one Homecoming Dance and one Sadie Hawkins Dance. I was shocked they didn't call again.

I didn't tell Ethel any of this because she seemed obsessed with talking about sex regardless, and had been like that long before I knew her. For years, my mother, Ethel's daughter, thought girls got pregnant if boys' tongues went into their mouths.

My mother grew up to become a nurse. My mother believed in science. When I asked how she ever bought the idea of spit-sperm, she said, "Your grandmother is not someone to argue with."

"They're only out for one thing," Ethel said about boys.

Ethel said, "That's how you happened, probably."

*　　　*　　　*

I never knew Ethel's husband, my grandfather. He died the year before my parents adopted me. He was an orphan, too. I've seen pictures—a tall thin man with dark eyes. He looked sad in his suspenders and fedora. His orphan story was different—his mother dropped him off at an orphanage when he was 10 because she couldn't afford him anymore.

"No shame in that," Ethel said.

Ethel had grown up poor, a child of the Depression. My grandfather had been born legitimate, with both a mother and father he knew. I was different.

There was no shame in being poor. The shame was sex.

"Some women don't know how to keep their legs closed," Ethel said.

In pictures, my grandfather looked plowed over by the world. I imagine all the years he spent with Ethel, that wall of sound.

"It's a shame he died before you came," Ethel said.

She said, "Maybe he would have known what to make of you."

*   *   *

I wouldn't read much into Ethel's behavior toward me for a long time. I didn't think about how adoption was probably a complicated problem for her. I didn't wonder what was underneath her insistence that, if he'd lived, maybe my grandfather would have loved me.

Ethel was my only living grandparent. I had a lot invested in our relationship. I was used to the way she hit me with the wooden spoon she kept near the stove, the way she chased me around the Polish Club kitchen and pulled my long blonde hair. I figured we were close enough to be cruel to one another.

It's easy, maybe, to mistake cruelty for honesty and to mistake honesty for love.

Sometimes I'd joke about getting Ethel a bikini. Sometimes I'd ask how many boys played with her boobs because they were big enough to rest a tray table on.

"Must be convenient on vacation," I said about her boob tray.

*　　　*　　　*

Even a meteor of a woman like Ethel has a nemesis, or at least a foil. For Ethel, it was Fanny. Next to my grandmother, Fanny looked like a toy person, something made of toothpicks and worn-out felt.

"Old Piss and Moan," Ethel named Fanny.

Every Wednesday, Fanny came to bingo and ordered her usual—fried fish sandwich, half a bun.

"And blot it good," Fanny would say, meaning she wanted the grease from the fish sopped with a paper towel before I served it to her.

"That Fanny gets my goat," Ethel said, her face turning red as the roses on her housedress. "She can go to hell."

Why Ethel was so furious with Fanny, I didn't know. Maybe there was history, maybe not. Maybe some friends hated each other. Maybe family did. I, the orphan, the adopted child, was still sorting people and their motives out.

*　　　*　　　*

Ethel and Fanny were neighbors. Ethel lived in a yellow house with two windows on the second floor and a white porch awning that made the house look like a duck. Fanny lived in a lopsided white box that seemed about to collapse down the ragged hill it was built upon.

The houses, like the women themselves, seemed like something from cartoons. Ethel — spastic, quacking. Fanny — some sad thing a wolf started to blow down.

Ethel used her capacity for joy as a weapon. She'd crank up Frankie Yankovic's "Beer Barrel Polka" in the kitchen and do a little two-step from the stove to the fryer and back.

Fanny complained. About everything.

"That's noise pollution," Fanny said about Ethel's music. "I can't hear them call the numbers over that racket."

"Drop dead already," Ethel said, and turned the music up more.

*   *   *

I didn't mind Fanny. I thought I knew something about sadness. I was drawn to it like a mirror. If Ethel believed in blood, I believed in the bonds between strangers.

"I want to narrow the gap of strangeness and alienation," Rod McKuen said about his purpose in the world.

"Here, let me help," I'd say and step toward Fanny, order pad in hand.

"I don't know how you can stand her," Ethel said to me about Fanny. Ethel said it like a challenge, like she was testing something, my loyalty maybe.

"You people are trying to kill me," Fanny said, and she meant Ethel and me and everyone else.

*   *   *

I didn't know how old Fanny was, but unhappiness carved her face and hands into canyons, things that take centuries to form. I never saw her smile.

"Give me one good thing to smile about," she said.

I tried. To make Fanny happy would be a triumph. It would mean I was a decent person worthy of love, maybe. I liked to create joy in other people. I liked the power of that, proof I had something to offer the world.

And so I told Fanny funny stories from the news, some neighborhood gossip. I shared the latest good-luck bingo trick I overheard. It usually involved a troll doll or a prayer to some obscure saint who specialized in gamblers and other lost souls.

Lately I saw a lot of St. Expeditus on glass candles and necklaces. Sometimes he was brunette, sometimes blonde, sometimes bald with an empty bowl balanced on his head. No one was sure he'd been a real martyr. His backstory was fishy—Roman soldier martyred in Turkey, beheaded, set on fire, fed to lions, tossed in the sea. One story went, the devil came to Expeditus disguised as a crow and tried to delay the would-be saint's conversion to Christianity. The crow cawed "tomorrow tomorrow" over and over. Expeditus, in a hurry to save his soul, shouted "No, today" and stomped the crow to death.

I told Fanny that story.

I said, "Expeditus. Expedite. Clever."

I said, "He's the go-to guy if you're desperate."

I said, "You have to run something in the paper for it to work."

Fanny looked like she needed to spit.

She said, "Everybody has a gimmick."

About me, she said, "They see you coming."

*   *   *

"Leave it be," my grandmother said. "Misery is as misery does."

"That Fanny," my grandmother said. "She loves to hang on her cross."

*   *   *

Every Wednesday, Ethel pretended Fanny wasn't standing in the Polish Club kitchen, ragged wallet out, demanding that Ethel serve her.

Every Wednesday, Fanny inched closer to Ethel, two planets bent on collision, until I put myself between them and took Fanny as my responsibility.

"All yours," Ethel said when she saw Fanny coming.

My grandmother would bow a little and say, "Be my guest."

*   *   *

One Wednesday, Fanny came in. Her dyed black hair curled like a raccoon on her head. Every week she seemed a little shorter, and this day the top of her head hit where my boobs would have been if I had them, if boys really had been doing the job of boob-groping Ethel believed they were born to do.

I had to stoop to look at Fanny. Her eyes, as usual, were red and runny, like she was allergic to the world, like she spent most of her downtime weeping. But to-day there was something charged about her, too. She looked alive. She shifted from side to side, like she was revving up. She ordered her fish, half a bun. Then she added. "And you stop pussyfooting around." Fanny pointed an arthritic finger up at me. It looked like a hook, like she wanted to gouge an eye out.

She said, "You know I can't have the grease."

She said, "You two are in cahoots."

~ 27 ~

Again she said, "You people are trying to kill me."

I must have somehow botched the grease-blotting, and Fanny thought I'd screwed her over. I was therefore responsible for a week's worth of burping and indigestion and all the unhappiness in Fanny's world.

Or it was more than that.

It was probably more than that.

I didn't know anything about Fanny's life, not really. I didn't know if she'd ever been married, if she had kids, if she did have kids where were they and so on. I didn't know what music she may have liked beyond polka noise pollution or what the inside of her sad little house looked like or if she had cereal in her cupboard or what toothpaste she used or if her teeth were mostly her own.

She may have had doilies on her tables.

Her house may have smelled like lemons.

I didn't know, and I didn't care, not really.

Empathy, like writing, can be about kindness or it can be an aggressive act, both. To assume to know things about strangers without really knowing them can be its own kind of violence. It's using other people as stand-ins. It comes across as something selfless, when it can be just the opposite.

"The light in me recognizes the light in you," the Buddhists say. "Namaste."

I don't think they have a word for recognizing sadness, though.

I knew I was sad. I didn't know if I was sad because I'd been born that way or because I'd been dropped into Ethel's family and didn't fit. I didn't know if I could fix myself or if I could bend to match the world that had taken me in. I didn't know how much it might hurt to do that.

Better to practice on Fanny, her sadness. If Fanny fell, I would still be standing.

"When you assume you make an ass out of you and not me," Ethel, who liked to tweak a cliché, would say.

St. Expeditus, help us.

St. Expeditus, get us the hell out of here.

"I'm on it," I said about Fanny's fish, and turned back to the fryer.

*   *   *

I spent nights lying on my pink-shag rug, my head wedged between two stereo speakers. I played "Seasons in the Sun" over and over and pondered how to get out of Trafford, this rusted mill town with its rigged bingo jackpots and a creek so polluted it turned everything it touched—rocks, tree roots, skin—orange.

Trafford—home to churches and funeral homes and dive bars with clever names like Warden's Bar and The Fiddle Inn.

"Get it?" Ethel said. "You fiddle in and you stumble out."

Trafford—home to my grandmother and Fanny and me.

*   *   *

"Anyone lived in a pretty how town," E. E. Cummings wrote.

"I'm nobody," Emily Dickinson wrote. "Who are you?"

"Temporary," people say about lives they're born or fall into and plan to fix.

*   *   *

Sometimes I still think about my Uncle Milton, the retired banker, who died alone in his house in Braddock. I was young when he died, maybe 10 or so. He was my dad's brother. I saw him at funerals, the occasional Christmas. He wore nice suits and smelled clean.

Uncle Milton was a bachelor. He loved money and the stocks and had a subscription to *The Wall Street Journal*, which my father said was expensive and something only a jackass like Milton would spend good money on.

Uncle Milton was dead for over a week before anyone noticed. The *Wall Street Journals* piled up on his porch. The mailman called the police to check it out.

I'd been in Uncle Milton's house a few times. It was dark, the furniture heavy and expensive-looking, the curtains heavy and expensive-looking. A gold-framed picture of Jesus's sacred heart hung on the wall. In the picture, Jesus's chest was split open. He held his heart in one hand. The heart was on fire. The heart was crowned with thorns. His other hand made the sign of peace, two fingers together, pointing up.

"All that money and he dies alone like that," my father said about his brother.

"Do you know who you have in this world?" my father would ask. Most times he'd let the question hang like that, a blank to fill in, something that should be obvious.

*   *   *

"One day anyone died I guess," wrote E. E. Cummings.

"Do you know who you have in this world?" my sad friend Louise would ask me many years later, and she'd answer, "Yourself."

*   *   *

If you want St. Expeditus's help, you must present him with an offering.

Pound cake, for instance.

*   *   *

Back at the fryer, I worked Fanny's fish as she stood by.

I made a big deal out of lifting it from the hot grease and letting it drip. I put it on a paper plate and let it rest there a bit. I took paper towels, a wad of them. I blotted. I blotted again. I blotted again.

There is so little we can do for one another in this world.

Fanny watched. I could feel her watching. Over on the stove, a pot of hot dogs boiled down. I tried not to think of Fanny like that, withered and curling into herself, the smell of hot-dog water on her breath.

In the background, I could feel Ethel watching too. I knew if I turned she would look disgusted. I knew she'd have her hands on her hips.

"Pain in my ass," she said under her breath, and then, louder, "That Fanny is a pain in mine."

I turned.

I looked at her as if to say, "Fanny likes to hang on her cross so let her hang."

My grandmother's laugh ricocheted around the room like a bullet.

"Get it Fanny?" she said. "You're a pain in my ass."

She said, "Fanny is a pain in my fanny."

Then my grandmother slapped her own huge ass. She held a pose, an index finger to her lips like "oops."

The flesh underneath Ethel's housedress quaked. Fanny looked like she might cry.

"It's okay," I said. "It's done."

I hurried things up. I tucked the fish into its bun and handed it over. Fanny inspected it. She pulled it close, then held it at arm's length, then close again.

"All right then," she said.

Then she tipped me a quarter.

This was 1982. A quarter could buy a phone call or some gum, and Fanny could pretend she didn't know but she did. I could tell by the way she gave it to me, like she was pinching my palm, like she hoped maybe the quarter would turn into a razor and make me bleed a little so I could know how it feels.

This made my grandmother laugh louder.

"Cheap is as cheap does," Ethel said as Fanny waddled off, holding the fish on the paper plate in front of her with both hands, like it was something holy, an offering on fire.

I'm not sure why I felt betrayed, but I did.

"Sometimes I think people were meant to be strangers," Rod McKuen said.

I put Fanny's quarter into Ethel's found money jar. Where I fit in the world, I didn't know.

Saint Expeditus, help me. Do this for me. Be quick.

As Fanny made her way out to the hall, I could hear her talking to everyone and no one. She said no one knew how she suffered. She said she couldn't bear it. She said if she wasn't careful, the grease would keep her up all night.

She said it was about her heart, which of course it was.

My friend Patience is a librarian. I'm a writer.

"Real James Deans," Patience calls us.

Patience and I did not grow up in families of readers. In our craggy Pennsylvania towns, it was better to be caught with a cigarette than a book. It was better for our mothers to catch us getting fingered by a boy than catch us on the couch reading.

Reading was uppity.

Reading made people think things.

"Devil's work," Patience's mother would say.

My mother called it lazy.

"Don't you have something useful to do?" she'd say, and mean dishes.

In Patience's house, there was a Bible and copies of *Highlights for Children* lifted from the dentist's office. There was *The Farmer's Almanac*. There was *TV Guide*.

Me, I kept a Webster's dictionary in the bathroom of my parents' pink one-story house. I hid it under the sink, behind stacks of toilet paper and my father's tubes of Preparation H. The dictionary's cover was denim blue, designed to look like the back pocket of a pair of jeans, an everyday thing.

My mother hated bathroom reading most of all.

"Shit or get off the pot," she'd say.

"The mouth on that one," my father, the mill worker, said when they fought. "Just like her mother."

I saw words as handed-down things, like heart disease and bad teeth.

Orphaned, adopted, I was not my parents' child.

I'd hide in the bathroom and read and memorize dictionary pages. I'd find smug new words and use them in sentences at dinner.

Words I liked: Flibbertigibbet. Oxymoron. Loquacious.

"I could wipe my ass with what you know," my father liked to say.

"I don't know where you came from," my mother would say, and I'd say, "Neither do I."

"I don't know where you came from," Patience's mother would say to her, too, though Patience was what my grandmother called a natural-born child.

I was not natural.

I was loved, mostly, despite it.

One time my father bought me a set of encyclopedias from a man who was selling them door-to-door. My father never opened the door for strangers, but this time he did. I don't know why. The set was *The World Book of Knowledge*. The books looked like Bibles, eggshell colored covers, gold spines, gold-tipped pages with strings sewn into the binding to use as bookmarks.

"She's smart," my father would say to explain why I'd hole up for hours reading A-C when my mother thought I should be outside playing.

"She'll ruin her eyes," my mother said.

"She'll go to college," my father said.

My father bought a bookshelf, the only one in the house, a low two-shelved number he put together just for the encyclopedias. The bookshelf had a glass door that slid closed to keep the books safe from dust.

My father wanted the books safe.

My mother wanted me safe from the books.

"I want what's mine to stay mine," my mother liked to say, something she learned from her father, an orphan like me. He meant he wanted his children close. He meant he didn't want anyone to leave him ever again.

"She'll get ideas," my mother would say about the encyclopedias and the worlds inside them.

My mother sighed a lot. She dusted the bookshelf with a pink feather duster. As far as I knew, she never opened any of the books.

Patience and I met in college. We were English majors. My mother told people I was going to be Barbara Walters.

"Pipe dreams," my mother said, and I imagined a pipe as big as a factory, an assembly-line of clouds.

I'm not sure how Patience's mother explained things.

When Patience was eight, an encyclopedia salesman came to her house, too. Albion, Pennsylvania, was farm country, tornado country, the kind of place where people name their children after virtues or deserts or saints. There were a lot of girls named Hope and Mary in Patience's school, and one girl named Sahara.

The day of the encyclopedia, the doorbell rang. Patience's mother, expecting vacuum cleaners or a new kind of floor soap, opened the door, and this man dressed for the city said, "Might I borrow a few moments of your time, Miss?"

Patience's mother looked more than her age.

She looked like a woman with housecoats and three children and a life in Albion, Pennsylvania. She looked like a woman who'd welcome the opportunity to purchase a new kind of floor soap and she knew it.

The man held up a big white book. The words *Wonderland of Knowledge* were embossed in gold on the cover and there was a picture of a globe, shiny blue for water, more gold for the land.

Patience peeked from behind her mother.

The man bent down. "Hello, honey," he said. "Do you like to read? I know I do."

Patience liked to read. Patience liked globes, too.

The man made a flourish, a magic trick. He tried to present the book to Patience's mother, who kept both hands on the doorframe.

"You'll be giving your beautiful daughter a head start," he said. "She'll have an advantage over other kids."

The *TV Guide* was open on the coffee table, dog-eared, highlighted, the map of the world that turned inside the console TV.

Patience's mother was proud of that TV, the sturdiest piece of furniture in the house.

"This will outlast me," she'd say, and pat the TV like a puppy.

Patience took care of both her parents until they died. Now she lives alone in a small apartment with a cat and many books, and says she doesn't like people though both of us know it's not true. Patience's car is filled with books on tape. When she drives, she turns up the volume and likes to feel the stories, those other worlds whirling inside her.

Back then, the salesman held his magic book like a lantern. Patience watched her mother once-over his shined shoes, tweed pants, smooth hands, gold watch big as a compass.

"Now why," she said, the words slow, clicking like deadbolts, "would my daughter deserve an advantage over anyone?"

THINGS TO REMEMBER

I worked at Things Remembered in Monroeville Mall the Christmas I was 17.

I was in love and needed money to buy my boyfriend one of those silver-plated ID bracelets they sold at Things Remembered. This was the 1980s and love meant personalizing things like yo-yos and ice cream scoopers, cheese boards and cheap jewelry.

I hoped my boyfriend would buy me an ID bracelet, too. I hoped he'd engrave his name on the back and sign it *all my love* and dot the i's in both our names with bubble hearts.

We'd hold up our identical wrists in Christmas Eve candlelight. We'd kiss the way people kiss in chewing gum commercials.

"A moment to remember," the Things Remembered catalogue would call it.

*   *   *

That Christmas, the mall was filled with fake snow. There was fake snow on the store windows and fake snow in my Orange Julius and fake snow on Monty the Talking Parrot's cage, despite the risk Monty might eat it and die.

Monty was stationed near the iron-on decal store. The smell of burning plastic and puffy paint probably wasn't good for him, either. It seemed cruel to leave him out in the open like that, but the mall had some fascination with live animal displays.

By the escalators was a wooden bridge over a small koi pond. The koi looked fat and warty, probably because kids kept trying to feed them pennies. Couples stopped on the bridge to pose for pictures. The mall was romantic like that.

As for Monty, I don't know how old he was, but he sounded like one of *The Golden Girls*, and his feathers fell out in clumps. Beneath his cage were piles of feathers that from a distance looked like more fake snow.

Monty would wish people happy holidays. He'd say, "Santa," and sound excited.

When children got too close to his cage, Monty would scream "Cops!"

*   *   *

My job was to stand for my six-hour shift and wear a Santa hat that drooped like a nut-sack.

I would not have said nut-sack back then because I had a lot invested in being a nice girl. I didn't smoke or drink or do drugs. I liked unicorns and black-velvet posters, and I believed when I did lose my virginity, it would be in a field of sunflowers.

I have never seen a field of sunflowers in Pittsburgh.

Who I was back then, I don't know.

*   *   *

My job was also to make duplicate keys and write names in glitter-glue on Christmas stockings.

"And remember our slogan," my sad middle-aged boss would say.

Things Remembered was going through a re-branding. People had a hard time remembering the name of

the store, according to corporate. They kept calling it Things to Remember.

People like me, the kiosk-faces of the company, were supposed to change that.

"Thanks for your business," I'd say and hand over a key I knew wouldn't work.

"People always remember you," I'd say, "when you shop at Things Remembered."

*   *   *

I was bad at slogans and key-making because I was nervous all the time. It's hard being a nice girl when you really want to say things like *nut-sack*.

My hands shook like the rabid animatronic squirrels that creeped the kids out over in Santaland. This meant I was also not a strong glitter-glue writer. The stockings I made were illegible. I'd try to write Bobby and it would come out Blobby and so forth. I compensated by adding more glitter and hoped no one would notice.

When customers walked away, a sparkling mess in their hands, they'd leave behind trails of glitter, paths out of a dark forest.

Sometimes I thought about following them home.

I'd say, "Remember me? From Things Remembered?"

*   *   *

My boss often left me alone in the kiosk. I liked that.

I could watch couples on their way to the koi-pond bridge or The Brown Derby restaurant, where they'd ask for window seats. They'd look out over the indoor ice rink and watch the skaters swirling like silk below, then order The Potato Wheel, fancy like that.

The Potato Wheel was a Lazy Susan filled with potato toppings. You could spin bacon bits, sour cream, chives and cheese. You could load up your potato with delight.

Where I'm from, we called this romance.

What I knew at 17: if a date took you to The Brown Derby, it meant something.

If a date ordered The Potato Wheel, it was love.

*   *   *

My Things Remembered boss hated the idea of love and the way the word seemed to be engraved on everything we sold.

Instead of focusing on sales, he spent a lot of time on his hair.

He held his comb-over in place with a can of Aqua Net he kept under the kiosk counter.

The glitter I'd send flying off stockings would catch in his sticky-do. I tried hard not to stare at his scalp, which was pink and shiny, like the belly of a seashell.

Glittered up, his scalp sparkled under the fluorescent lights. It looked pretty.

*   *   *

My boss did not glitter. He hated many things we sold, but he hated the mizpahs most.

Mizpah necklaces split in half. Lovers and best friends and mothers and daughters give mizpahs to each other. The classics have the words "The LORD (all caps) watch between me and thee when we are absent one from another." Others just had the word Forever, with the jagged slash between the For and the Ever.

Mizpahs were our best sellers. My boss found this insulting.

"You know these things were originally about war?" he liked to tell customers and me. "Mizpah means watchtower. A mizpah was something enemies set up after a truce to make sure they didn't screw each other over."

He said, "It's funny when you think about it."

He said, "Between me and thee."

"Forever," he said. "Now isn't that some hippy-dippy shit."

*   *   *

I didn't know much about my boss, but he reminded me of my driver's ed teacher.

My driver's ed teacher was depressed. He was going through a divorce. The divorce made him not care about things like teaching teenagers how to drive.

When I'd blow through a yellow light or nearly get sideswiped on the cloverleaf off-ramp on Route 30, he'd sigh.

"Everything's temporary, kid," he'd say, and I thought he meant my driver's permit.

*   *   *

At 17, I believed in forever. I believed I'd always be in love with my nice boyfriend, even though we didn't have a lot in common.

We did both like Billy Joel and anchovies and Trivial Pursuit. When we won a round in Trivial Pursuit, we both liked to yell "Pie Me!" and were the only ones who thought that was funny.

Otherwise, there wasn't much between us.

I figured love was like that for most people.

I figured love lasted despite people.

LORI JAKIELA

*   *   *

At 17, I wanted to see the world as beautiful and I did.

At middle age, my boss wanted to see the world as terrible and he did.

To believe in people and love requires suspension of disbelief.

Middle-aged now, I can barely remember myself at 17. I can barely remember myself at last week.

The author Haven Kimmel says we all carry our younger selves in us all the time. "It's your acorn," Haven says about it. "You grow around yourself like a tree."

*   *   *

Maybe Things Remembered was a corporate version of a playground tree everyone wanted to carve names on.

Maybe we wanted something metal and solid to say we were here, we loved each other, and maybe that mattered a little.

Or maybe it was just an easy way to make people think we'd spent a lot of time worrying over them, their gifts.

Maybe it was a way to make people think we were very clever and creative and that we cared more than we did.

"It's hard to tell baloney from real beer," my boss used to say.

I didn't know what he meant by that. My boss was old, 40 at least. I figured to people of his generation, things like baloney and beer meant something.

*   *   *

When he'd get drunk, my friend Joe would pick fights with inanimate objects in bars, ashtrays mostly.

"This piece of plastic will outlive me," he'd say. "It will outlive me and you and everyone we know."

He'd say, "Fuck you, ashtray."

That's the power of things.

*   *   *

My long-ago boyfriend is happily married now, I think. Facebook says he has kids and a dog and loves The Steelers.

I am happily married, with two kids and two fish. The fish are jerks, but everything else is good.

I'm a writer. Writing allows me to remember things. There's power in remembering, maybe.

"I can't go on," Brendan Behan says. "I go on."

*   *   *

"Love you," I said to my boyfriend that Christmas Eve when I slipped the ID bracelet on his wrist.

I'd made it myself, so the writing on the metal was ragged, like I'd written it with my toes.

My boyfriend slipped the ID bracelet he'd gotten me at some other Things Remembered onto my wrist.

Within a month, it will turn my wrist green and my boss will look at it and say, "He didn't splurge for the silver-plate. Isn't that some shit?"

But in the moment, in the candlelight I'd imagined, my boyfriend said it back. "Love you."

It's what he'd written on the bracelet, too. *Love you.* Not "I love you." *Love you.* A hope, a wish.

"A gift that inspires," the Things Remembered catalogue would say.

Love you.

As in *Someone, someday will.*

I'm into Leather

The sign for Chief's Café in Pittsburgh was a neon fireman's hat and hose. Someone threw a rock through the right side of the sign and smashed it up, but it still glowed and buzzed like an electric snake. I guessed the owner was a fire chief. I guessed this was the kind of place someone who lived for emergencies built.

I hung out at Chief's because I was 26 and trying to be a poet, and beer at Chief's was cheap, and I liked to drink when I had poet-emergencies over heartbreaks and line-breaks and bitchy form-poets who counted syllables by whacking pencils against their teeth.

Chief's was not a formal-poet place. Chief's was a barfly place where the bartender doled out bags of barbecue pork rinds and wore a cowboy hat that looked like it had just been punched.

When I say I was trying to be a poet, I mean I was in graduate school. I was a scholarship kid, on a teaching assistantship. This meant I didn't have to pay to study poetry, which is why such a thing was possible. Before this, not long before this, I hadn't known they gave people degrees to write poems. I was working in public relations at a college when a poetry professor with many scarves and turquoise rings befriended me. I thought she was joking when she suggested poem-school.

"That's ridiculous," I said. "Nobody does that."

"I did that," she said and looked hurt, though she walked me through the application process anyway.

And now, against all odds, here I was. It wasn't going well. One night, after a particularly bad workshop, and a nice round of pity-partying myself, I called my friend Felix and he agreed to meet me at Chief's if I promised to pay for the beer.

"As many as it takes," he said when I picked him up at his apartment in Homestead, and I said, "At least."

Felix was a poet-slash-performance artist. He had performed his poems on MTV and once off-Broadway in the nude. Sometimes, when he had money, he and some friends rode around in a van that looked like they beat it with hammers. "We bring poetry to the people," Felix said, and he sounded like Whitman, though the van thing was probably more like banging on a can in the subway for beer money.

Felix called himself a street poet.

"That's just fucked up," Felix said about universities teaching people to write poems.

My family agreed.

"At least you'll be able to write something on those signs you'll be holding up," my cousin Jeff said.

Jeff had a little Hitler mustache. His face was a fist I wanted to bump with a truck.

"Will Rhyme for Food," Jeff said, and made like he was putting it on a t-shirt.

I hated him.

I hated my poetry professor, too, which was what this was all about.

"She says my poems lack emotion and meaning," I told Felix. I faked a British accent and pretended to peer over bifocals, even though the professor in question was from Las Vegas and did not wear glasses and she said her perfect vision was a metaphor for the poet's gaze.

"One must see well to truly see," she said, like it was another thing to put on a t-shirt, a very expensive one.

*   *   *

When I first came to graduate school, I showed up in a puffy-paint sweatshirt I bought in Key West. Like all things Key West—key chains, shot glasses, ass-less chaps—the sweatshirt had a picture of Hemingway on it. I thought Hemingway would make me look literary. I thought Hemingway would help me make friends. I was new and scared, but I'd read every book Hemingway published, which meant I'd read enough Hemingway to know Hemingway would hate having his head on puffy-paint sweatshirts.

Still, I figured reading that much Hemingway should count for something.

"Cute shirt," a Ph.D. student I didn't know said.

I was going to say thank you when I realized she was being ironic.

Irony is the language of graduate school. I was just learning to tune my ears and brain to it. Years before, I'd have called Ph.D. a bitch. Years later, I'll call her snarky. In this moment, I was supposed to call her a Deconstructionist while quoting French theorists whose names sounded like farts.

Ph.D. pointed at my chest, then brought her finger up fast to flick my nose. I looked down at my shirt, how big it was, the rolls of blue cotton sagging around my waist and breasts, the toxic smell wafting up from Hemingway's beard.

"Just so you know," Ph.D. said. "Hemingway was a racist, misogynist, homophobic asshole and the patriarchy is d-e-a-d DEAD."

Then she spun on her pink combat boots and stomped off, thrift-store hippie skirt wafting behind like incense.

*   *   *

I used to think I would fit in among my own people — writer people, book people — and that things would be different than they were back home with my cousin Jeff. I used to think books and reading made people kinder, gentler. I used to think books made people better, that books would make me better, but there's only so much books can do.

*   *   *

Back at Chief's, Felix and I sat at the bar, a stack of ones and some quarters in front of me, exact change plus tips. Felix rubbed his nose, then swirled a finger in his beer, the salt from his skin taking the head down to nothing.

"I mean if my poems lack both meaning and emotion, head and heart, what do they have?" I asked Felix, over and over, until his eyes went limp, until he started playing with his dreads. He pulled them to his nose, one after another, like he was checking to see if he smelled like smoke because everything in Chief's smelled like smoke, down to the smeared beer glasses and fake wood paneling.

The guy next to us, who smelled like smoke and looked like a chicken cutlet, his skin breaded in sand and dirt and peanut oil, said "Poets." He said, "Fuck." He said, "I should write a book." He said, "You think you know some shit? I know some shit."

The floor beneath him was covered with the fluff and sawdust he'd picked out of his slashed red vinyl seat. Most of the seats in Chiefs were slashed and I figured everybody in there had a knife but me.

"I know this one guy. He brought a bowie knife to one of those workshops once," Felix said. "He didn't say anything, just plopped the knife down, wham, like that on the table and gave it a little twirl, like he was spinning a bottle, like he was waiting to be kissed. Nobody said anything to him after that."

"I don't think that would work for me," I said, but I thought about Ralph's Army Surplus, where I bought my black turtlenecks. I thought about Ralph's collection of knives behind glass and the Semper Fidelis flag hung over the counter and the retired Marine clerk who liked to talk about how he used to train grunts in Vietnam by hitting them over the heads with two-by-fours.

"What you need," Felix said, "is a way to get people to stop fucking with you. You need a front." Then he took off his leather jacket and handed it over.

"I've always loved the Ramones," I said and pumped my fist.

Felix said, "Fuck the Ramones. Put that on. It's yours. At least wear it to that workshop. You'll look tougher if you lose that secretary hair."

I ran a hand through the tangles of my blonde perm, which up until that minute I'd thought was OK—wild even.

I said, "Are you serious?"

About the jacket, I said, "It's too much," even though I was already putting it on, even though it felt instantly right, even though the leather was a little squeaky and the studs on the collar a little big and the whole thing smelled like it had been through a fire, a fire that maybe Felix set because Felix was violent and troubled in ways I refused to think about.

*   *   *

Felix and I wanted to be deep, believed we were deep. Twenty years later, I realize I no longer care about deep, can no longer define deep, could give a shit about deep. Twenty years later I know deep never existed. I have a husband now, and two kids, and four books. I know exactly who I am at most moments, and the people I love remind me the other times. It would take me years — maybe until this second — to realize how little I knew about Felix.

The stories he told bounced off my permed hair and my stupid poems and the leather jacket and echoed like every other story I'd heard, a little sadder, maybe, but still a story, another line from another poet that was probably true but maybe not.

Felix's dad beat him, I think. I know his mom wasn't around. He wanted to go on tour with Lolla-palooza. He wanted to meet Nirvana. He was friends with Ani Difranco. He was diabetic. He liked cats but was allergic, so he left milk out for strays. One time, stoned at my apartment, he jacked off in the bathroom and wiped it on my roommate's monogrammed towels. I thought he was gross, like a person who doesn't shower, not like a rapist. So I didn't invite him to our apartment. But I still met him at bars. Gross was fine for bars.

One time he asked me to hold a big Ziploc bag of weed in our freezer for him. I didn't do it, even though he said if I did I could take whatever I wanted. I don't know why I didn't do it any more than I understood why I did the things I did.

~ 50 ~

Also, I really liked pot.

"Take whatever you want," he said. "It doesn't matter how much you take."

When I said sorry, no, Felix stored his weed somewhere else and gave me free joints anyway, and my life went along easy like that.

So Felix was as shallow as I. He was worse. I liked worse. I could take from someone who was worse. I could also take from someone who was cool. I get confused remembering how stupid I was.

Felix never called me on how much I took. His weed. His time. His jacket. His friendship. That's not really friendship. Taking without giving is a shitty thing to do, but I kept on. Felix's giving without taking was something else — an emptying out, maybe.

About the jacket, I said, "Thank you. Holy shit."

I caught a glimpse of myself in the metal bar posts. I caught a glimpse in the greasy bar mirror. I squinted and turned and felt, maybe for the first time, inexplicably myself, even if I was the punchline my cousin Jeff had been hoping for all those years.

I was pushing 30 and dressed like The Fonz.

I wrote terrible poems, but I wanted to write better ones.

As a writer, I believed form followed content.

As a person, I was the other way around.

"Build it and they will come," somebody told Kevin Costner in that movie *Field of Dreams*. I was building myself so the life I wanted would come.

Felix was, I think, disassembling, though I was too lost in myself to notice.

*   *   *

"Thank you," I said again to Felix, like he'd given me a kidney.

He clicked his tongue against his teeth. He held his hand out to say stop. He looked almost vulnerable in his black t-shirt and jeans, like without his jacket he was mortal, just blood and skin.

Felix said, "It's nothing."

He said, "Beer me."

*   *   *

A few weeks after Felix gave me the jacket, I woke up with a Carlo Rossi hangover, a bad case of whiplash, and a bass player named Bix in bed beside me. Bix was naked and sprawled like Jesus on the cross, arms out, feet together in a twist. I was shoved to the edge of the bed, bare mattress against my cheek. I was wearing Bix's Nirvana t-shirt. There were brown crumbs all over the sheets and in Bix's scraggly chest hair.

I had a vague memory of Bix, already drunk and stoned, slipping a tab of cartoon-Santa acid on his tongue, then making gingerbread from a box and feeding it to me with his fingers. The whiplash, I figured, was from the slam-dancing I'd done the night before, when Bix's band played at The Electric Banana and did a rocking cover of "Kung Fu Fighting."

Bix's hair was splayed over two pillows. By the time he woke up, it was well past noon, which meant he was late and going to have to explain to his live-in girlfriend where he'd been. Bix had rock-star hair. Bix loved his rock-star hair. I think Bix's rock-star hair was the only thing I liked about him, too, but stress made Bix's hair fall out in clumps.

"I have a condition," he said, in the same way an 80-year-old man might talk about his goiter. Bix creaked out of bed, tenderly rolled his hair into a Rasta cap without combing it, then scooped the one remaining hunk of gingerbread out of the pan he'd stashed under the bed. Explaining to his live-in girlfriend where he'd been would be stressful, so after Bix left, I would have to vacuum up the hairballs that made a ghost-town tumbleweed path from my bed to the door. On his way out, Bix said in his swollen, phlegm-throated romantic way, "Let's hang out later."

I'd like to say this is the moment when I started to re-evaluate my life. Instead, I plugged in the vacuum cleaner and got to work. I ran the vacuum back and forth until Bix's hair jammed the motor and I smelled burning.

*   *   *

I met Bix and guys like him through my best friend, Sasha. Bix was not Sasha's fault. Sasha did not approve of my taste in men. They were simply a by-product of the world she and I inhabited, full of artists and Bohemians and misfits who worked hard to be misfits and, of course, douchebags. "There are some sounds only dogs can hear," Bix said when he was philosophically stoned, a metaphor for himself and other artists too deep to be understood by the average human.

Sasha smoked Salem Slim Lights and twirled them movie-star-style between tiny red-tipped fingers. She read Tarot cards. She knew her way around liquid black eyeliner. She drank too much and wore low-rise jeans and lacy black bra-tops and she was wonderful. She was also a painter, but her boyfriend Ed headed up the band Bix was in. The band was called The Frampton Brothers, and Ed, a genetic splice of Peter Frampton and Kenny G., was the perfect front man. These days, Sasha had given up on painting, mostly because Ed didn't like the paintings she'd done of past boyfriends. Ed kept Sasha busy designing his CD covers and band posters instead.

"The woman's got skills," Ed said.

Sasha was happy to help out. Still, I worried about her beautiful paintings wrapped up in garbage bags and hidden behind her couch. She and I often blew all our laundry quarters playing the Ramones on a juke-box in Jack's bar and talked about this. Sasha had plans — to get a better job, then a nicer apartment, one where she could have a studio just big enough for her easel and paints, not a guitar or amp in sight.

"This is just for now," she said.

And I said, "You're an artist. You have to paint. You have to be true to who you are."

I was a hypocrite, of course. I never talked to my musician boyfriends about writing. I played a good groupie, leather jacket and all. I played a good writer, sidled up to the bar at Chief's, but I'd written only one poem in the last three weeks. I'd written it over and over. I'd gone to nine rock shows instead. I stood in the dark and pretended to smoke and leaned in my black clothes against black painted walls and willed myself to disappear.

Semper fidelis, the old Marine at Ralph's would say, then spit.

*   *   *

Even though I wished things could be different for Sasha, I did like Ed's band. I understood why their single, "Dwarf Bowling," was a hit in both Japan and

Germany. This may be why I went along for the seven-hour drive to Hoboken, New Jersey, for the band's biggest CD-release party ever. This party marked the launch of *Bonograph: Sonny Gets His Share*, a compilation album that featured hip bands covering Sonny Bono's greatest hits like "Bang Bang (My Baby Shot Me Down)" and "Pammie's on a Bummer." The whole thing was Ed's idea. It featured REM's touring guitarist Peter Holsapple, the Flat Duo Jets, and Ed's band. The project had been featured on MTV and CNN. It made *People* magazine.

"It's going to devastate them," Ed said, and he meant critics. He meant *Bonograph* was going to be huge.

And so Sasha and I loaded up her paneled station wagon with plastic cups and screw-top wine to toast what we were certain would be a gateway to superstardom. "Finally all this will be worth it," Sasha said, and waved a Salem Slim Light around like a wand, like she was illuminating every dark corner of her life by showing the interior of this 1970s sit-com car she'd inherited from her parents and which now smelled like beer and sweat and feet and had been stolen once, but then found, abandoned somewhere in the Hill District. The thieves had taken some of Ed's equipment — amplifiers etc. — and left behind an empty can of peas.

"What kind of person eats cold peas out of a can?" Sasha wanted to know, as if this could explain everything.

*   *   *

"Pipe dreams" — my family's phrase for when people tried to imagine lives other than the ones they were born into. When my mother or my cousin or my grandmother said it, I imagined puffs of smoke, the hookah-loving caterpillar in "Alice in Wonderland" perched on the mushroom that could make Alice grow or shrink, depending.

"Who are you?" the caterpillar wanted to know. "Who do you think you are?"

Sasha and I had pipe dreams. They were as follows: we would make it out of Pittsburgh and get cars that wouldn't break down. I'd write, she'd paint, Ed would go on playing his music, Bix would go into rehab, I'd find a nice semi-drug-free guy with hair that stayed attached to his head, and we'd all move to New York, hang out in cafes, and be happy, the end.

"Here's to better things," Sasha said, a sappy song-lyric toast.

She cracked open our gallon of Carlo Rossi. We lied down in the back of the station wagon, and drank our way to Maxwell's, a nightclub smack in the middle of Frank Sinatra's old neighborhood.

"Whatever gets you through, baby," Sinatra used to say.

*　　　*　　　*

When we got to Maxwell's, many *Bonograph* stars, including REM's Holsapple, were already inside, and rumors were static-ing through the crowd that scouts from major labels were there, too. The air crackled with feedback and possibility. It was probably very exciting, but Sasha and I were already drunk.

Once inside the club, we commandeered two bar stools, an ashtray, and a basket of peanuts. We didn't move except for the occasional bathroom run.

At one point, a man with a ragged Beatles haircut and nice eyes leaned between us and said, "You two are so serious. What are you talking about? Smile, already!"

I have always hated people who tell me to smile. It's pushy, and an order is a horrible pickup line, but this man seemed kind. Besides, he had a Polaroid camera. It's impossible to resist a Polaroid camera. So Sasha and I leaned together, both of us in our leather jackets, and played it up. Sasha wore her biker hat. My blonde secretary hair was now cut short and slicked back.

"Cock your hat," Sinatra used to say. "Angles are attitudes," and we tried to look cool, tough, pursing our red lips and mugging for the camera here in Sinatra's hometown, but we couldn't hold out. Soon we beamed and the camera snapped and there we were, full of sweet cheap wine and joy in that dark and beautiful place.

We didn't know then that the guy with the camera was famous. We'd learn later, from the bartender, that the man was Peter Buck from REM. Years later, Ed would say we're crazy, that it was probably Holsapple, but I've looked at pictures of Peter Buck and this is the man I remember.

Back at Maxwell's, Peter Buck told us he was going down the block for a slice. He asked if we were hungry, if we wanted him to bring something back. He seemed like a neighborhood guy, about as far from a rock star as you could get.

*   *   *

What did we know?

"If the desire for the light is strong enough, the desire itself creates the light." Simone Weil said that.

Simone Weil died at 34. She joined the French Resistance and starved herself out of compassion for soldiers

LORI JAKIELA

who were dying of hunger. Albert Camus called her the one great spirit of his time. She was, more or less, a saint.

Sasha and I did not want to be saints. We didn't think about compassion, although it would have done us good to do so. We wanted to be artists and decent people. We wanted to be beautiful and good and wise, but we weren't anything, not yet.

We didn't know anything, not yet.

*   *   *

We didn't know, for instance, I'd be the one to end up in New York. I'd be a flight attendant. It would not be glamorous. I would not become a writer in New York. It would take love and family and coming back home to Pittsburgh to do that.

We didn't know nice Peter Buck would one day be arrested for getting drunk on an airplane and throwing yogurt at flight attendants like me.

We didn't know Ed would go to work for a newspaper and be known as a music critic more than a musician.

We didn't know Sasha would never get back to painting, but would marry Ed, move to the desert, and stockpile paints on the sly.

We could have guessed Bix would be a balding rehab dropout and simply disappear.

*   *   *

Felix ended up in Europe, where he was sure he could become a famous performance poet.

"They take art seriously over there," he'd tell me before he left. "Their poets are like fucking rock stars."

Felix emptied all the way out, then tried to kill someone, a blonde woman with secretary hair and a sweet smile who was trying to be a poet, too.

I was shallow and didn't try to kill anyone. Felix was shallow, so I assumed he wouldn't try to kill anyone. I didn't know he'd use a knife. I didn't know the woman would live.

I didn't know Felix would kill himself instead, overdosing on insulin.

He'd call me first, collect.

Years later I wouldn't remember anything he said.

PART 2

The author's view from the cockpit, circa 1995.

I Felt Like Licking Might Happen a Lot

I worked as a flight attendant for seven years, probably 5460 flights. I've said *hey* and *goodbye*, *Coke or Diet Coke*, and *tray-table-up-please* to about 546,000 people. 546,000 people is more than the entire population of Tulsa, Oklahoma.

Tulsa is famous for The Golden Driller, the biggest free-standing statue in the world, though the driller is more yellow-mustard than golden. He's ripped and cocky and has a massive belt buckle that says TULSA. He has his own oil derrick to lean on. Tourists stand under the statue and get pictures of themselves staring up at his impressive golden crotch.

*   *   *

I flew from 1994 until 2001. The weirdest in-flight story was the one about an investment banker from my home-base New York City.

On a flight from Buenos Aires to JFK, the banker got drunk. Flight attendants cut him off. The banker got angry. He helped himself to the liquor cart, stumbled to first-class, climbed on a service cart, dropped his pants, and, in front of everyone, took a shit. Then he stepped in his shit and tracked it through the cabin.

No flight attendant I've known ever questioned the story, even before it made international news, even before the banker had to cough up a $5,000 fine and 300 hours of community service and reimburse over $50,000

LORI JAKIELA

to the other passengers who had paid good airfare not to watch him shit on a service cart.

The only thing every flight attendant wanted to know was this: if the guy was so drunk, how did he get up on the cart? And how did he hold his balance once he was up there?

*   *   *

One time, professional wrestler Jake the Snake handed me his bag, then told me his pet python was inside.

I saw him in a movie once and all he wanted to do was cocaine.

Another guy zipped a Chihuahua into his jacket pocket, then put the jacket on the screening belt when he went through security. Two TSA agents saw the tiny skeleton and called Security, who escorted the guy and his dog off the plane.

*   *   *

During beverage service, a fat guy in suspenders snuck up and licked me. He nailed my neck, behind my right ear, in the little gap between my regulation scarf and my hairline.

I will always be traumatized by this.

He wasn't wearing shoes.

He had on red socks.

People who take their shoes off on airplanes are terrible people. (If this is you, I apologize. But please, put your shoes on.)

Shoeless people who lick flight attendants are worse.

All I could think to say was, "You. Step back. Now." I wiped the wet spot with my scarf and kept pouring drinks.

I didn't report it. It was embarrassing and I was pretty new. I felt like licking might happen a lot.

It didn't.

*   *   *

Passengers bicker and slap each other over arm rests. They fistfight for overhead space. They tattle on each other for cell phones and tray tables and seatbelts that need buckling.

They want upgrades. They want free round-trip tickets, free drinks, one of those turkeys the airline used to give out at Thanksgiving.

*   *   *

One day, a Furby malfunctioned and smack-talked Furbish from inside a little girl's backpack. The mother was embarrassed, exhausted. She mouthed "sorry, sorry," to all the other passengers who scowled as she took the Furby out of the backpack and tried to get it to stop.

She couldn't get it to stop. She needed a screwdriver to pop the batteries. Screwdrivers are weapons and not allowed on board.

A woman huffed and slammed her head into her seatback. A man hit his call button.

I took the Furby and wrapped it in a blanket. I stuffed it into the overhead where it was muffled to a nub.

People complained. They said they could still hear it. It was giving them headaches. It was making them crazy.

"I did not pay good money to listen to that garbage," the seatback woman said. She wanted a free ticket. She wanted free drinks.

I brought her drinks.

Then I brought drinks to everyone, including a bottle of champagne for the little girl's mother, who looked like she could use a drink most of all.

*   *   *

It's not okay to poke a flight attendant in the ass like the ass is a doorbell that might be broken.

It's not appropriate to do this even if you want to know what time it is in Iceland.

*   *   *

The first time I saw passengers try to have sex, it was a low-key thing, the back row in coach, not too crowded. The girl was giving the guy head. She was kneeling between the seats, buried in his lap.

"Excuse me," I said, "Can I get you both something to drink?"

Nothing.

"Would you like a snack?" I said.

I went back to the galley. Della, a senior flight attendant was there. I asked her what I should do.

"Cinderella," she said. Della called all junior flight attendants Cinderella. "You have to learn."

Della walked over to the couple, threw a blanket over them, and let them be.

"My dear," Della said, adjusting her scarf, "some things we don't get paid enough to do."

*   *   *

On a flight from New York to Boston, a group of kids were headed for tennis camp. The overheads were loaded with rackets and the kids all looked like they popped from a J.Crew catalog.

~ 66 ~

On descent, something went wrong with our hydraulics, which control the flaps, which steer the plane and help it slow down on landing. The captain, blonde and blow-dried, all starch and chisel, popped from the same J.Crew catalog as the kids, briefed the flight attendants. We prepared for an emergency landing.

The flight attendant I was working with was the meanest person I'd met. She was all muscle and bitch. Everything about her was short: her height, her hair, her temper.

"Fuck these people," she'd said before boarding, like she planned for everyone to have the shitty day it turned out to be.

When I looked at her, I saw a desiccated chicken wing.

I thought, I will not die next to a chicken wing.

Still, Chicken Wing and I showed people how to brace. We pointed out exits, explained what would happen if we had a hard landing, which is what we said instead of crash.

The people in the emergency exits froze.

A woman started talking loudly about her cat Sniggles.

Half the kids started throwing up.

The other half kept chanting, "We're going to crash in the ocean, we're going to crash in the ocean."

We didn't crash in the ocean.

In Boston, they gave us a long runway and foamed it down. There were fire trucks, ambulances. The plane made it to a full stop, and the captain came over the PA to let everyone know things were okay.

The woman with the cat started crying.

The emergency exit row people defrosted.

The kids who were throwing up stopped.
The kids who were chanting were disappointed.
They made a new chant. It went: "Aw."

* * *

I don't know why anyone would want to have sex on an airplane. It's cramped. The seats are uncomfortable. The lavs are disgusting. At any minute oxygen masks can fall from the ceiling.

Everything is inexplicably sticky on airplanes — maybe because people keep insisting on having sex in the sky, maybe because having sex in the sky makes them feel they can go on breathing.

Rough Air

"New Yawk to Hot-Lanta," the gate agent in his red coat drawls over the PA. His voice, all swamp and grits, sloshes down the jetway to where I'm standing, sneaking drags off the coffee I have stashed behind the galley wall.

It's 5:30 a.m., first flight out of LaGuardia, and I'm miserable. The red coat's name is Gary. He works a lot of my flights. Even though my name is on his departure reports and on my wings, he never uses it. Gary calls me Darling. He calls me Sugar. Sometimes, Hey Mama.

I hate him.

Maybe underneath the polyester coat and the dyed black comb-over, Gary is a nice guy, but I can't stand his jokes.

"What's the most important part of a head flight attendant's uniform? The knee pads!"

I hate how happy he is when he loads up an airplane full of drunks, then tells me to have a nice flight.

This morning, before he starts boarding, Gary sticks his head in the door and yells, "Ready or not, y'all, here they come!"

*   *   *

Gary loves to push a flight. All gate agents do. They'd use electric prods on passengers and flight attendants if it would help them set on-time records and earn them the company's coveted Feather in Your Cap award.

The Feather in Your Cap award is, literally, a feather glued to a piece of paper. No raise. No night on the town. No Delta Dream Vacation. Just a feather — which looks suspiciously pigeon-like — with the words GOOD JOB! HERE'S A FEATHER IN YOUR CAP.

*   *   *

This morning, when Gary says, "Ready or not," I say, "not" and wave him off. I'm in a mood. I'm nearly always in a mood on early-morning flights when passengers come on board exhausted and pissed off. They demand Asiago omelets and cappuccinos when they know they'll get a cookie and crappy airplane coffee with powdered creamer if they're lucky.

I say, "Good morning. Welcome aboard."

They say, "I'll have the omelet," or, on later flights, "I'll have the lobster."

I smile and say, "Good one" or "That sounds perfect" or "I think I'll join you." I smile again, a big landslide that smothers other things I want to say.

There are so many other things I want to say. But there are those pesky rules, regulations. Just as passengers must never say bomb when passing security, flight attendants are forbidden to use words like crash or otherwise incite fear in our on-board guests. When passengers give me a hard time about putting their tray tables up, I'm tempted to explain that, in the event of impact, tray tables work like guillotines, neatly slicing whatever's behind them in two.

During cabin safety announcements, flight attendants never say, "If there's an explosion." We say, "In the unlikely event of a sudden decompression."

We say, "Breathe normally."

We do not use words like storm, tornado, hurricane.

We say, "We are experiencing weather."

We don't say "turbulence." We call it "rough air."

*　　　*　　　*

Gary sends them down at five forty, early as usual, and I yawn through my welcomes, suck on an Altoid, and hope my lipstick hasn't bled onto my teeth. I've just heard my voice say, "An omelet? How perfect!" when I see this tiny woman halfway up the jetway, wrestling with a shoulder bag.

The woman looks about seventy. She is tiny, dainty, lace and flowers on her dress, a little hat topping her perfect ringleted hair. The bag keeps throwing her off balance as she bumps toward the plane, into other passengers who harrumph or say, "Excuse me" or just look generically mean.

When I say the woman is tiny, I mean the flower on the brim of her hat hits below my shoulder. I bend down and ask if she needs help.

"I don't want to be any trouble, honey," she says. "Don't want a fuss now."

I lift the bag and sling it over my shoulder, even though I've been trained not to do this. "Lift passenger bags at your own risk," the training manual says.

*　　　*　　　*

Airlines try to save money by cutting on-the-job injuries, so nearly everything passengers want flight attendants to do — maneuver a beverage cart, perform the Heimlich maneuver when someone chokes on a pretzel, restrain drunks and fellow flight attendants when they want to jettison the emergency slides — is at our own risk.

Once, shortly after I started flying, there was a storm and our plane was hit by lightning. There had been little warning—no calls from the cockpit, just bumps and dips, the usual rough air—and so I was in the aisle when there was a flash, then a loud bang. The plane dropped, like an elevator might if someone cut the cable, and I ended up on the floor six rows from where I'd been standing. I strapped myself into the nearest passenger seat and had to climb over a man to do it. "Don't you have your own seats in the back of the plane?" he said.

I was shaken, but not badly hurt. Another flight attendant in the plane's lower galley, though, had been pinned by a loose beverage cart. Beverage carts, when they're full, weigh more than 200 pounds. By the time I made it to the galley, she was lying on the floor. Another flight attendant was trying to calm her down. I'd never seen anyone convulse and it was terrifying. The woman's whole body spasmed and she made strange sounds, high-pitched, deep in her throat. When we landed, paramedics took her off through the cabin service door on a stretcher. When they moved her, she screamed.

Later, a supervisor came on board and interviewed the rest of us. Was the seat belt sign on? Did we think it was safe to be up? Shouldn't all the carts have been locked down?

The supervisor built the company's argument. The flight attendant should have been seated, the carts locked in place. She was irresponsible. She had been working at her own risk.

*   *   *

Back on the Hotlanta flight, I shift under the weight of the woman's bag. It feels loaded with bowling balls. I don't know how she's managed it this far and tell her so.

"Oh, I try and manage what I can," she says. "A girl needs a lot of makeup at my age." She winks, then adds, "Don't want to be no trouble, really now."

Just a week before, a woman named Marge struggled to stuff a bag like this one into the overhead and nearly knocked out another passenger sitting underneath. He was nailed with the corner of what turned out to be a bag filled with frozen meatballs, two roasts and a meatloaf. I had to fill out paperwork that said just that. The passenger was fine, but he wanted a free round-trip ticket and maybe one of those free Easter hams the airlines used to give out back when airlines used to care about people.

"Turkeys," I told him.

"What?" he said.

"The airlines used to give out turkeys. For Thanksgiving. Not Easter."

"Whatever," he said.

As for Marge's bag, it took two of us, plus Marge, to stow it under an empty seat in the back of the plane. Marge was headed to Fort Lauderdale to visit her daughter.

"My daughter," Marge said, shoving the bag with her foot. "She likes my cooking."

*   *   *

Did I say it's March? That means New York is a slag pile, all muck and slush. How nice it would be for someone to show up in March dragging a bag of meatballs, or to wake up with the sun in Ft. Lauderdale, where everything smells like strawberry lip gloss.

On all our family drives from Pittsburgh to Florida, my father taught me long ago that Florida was a working-class dream. It was the reason people killed themselves every day at jobs they hated for two weeks' vacation a year. It was where nearly everyone I knew wanted to go to die.

*   *   *

Sometimes I think I'd be happier if I transferred to Florida. I told this to Marlena, a flight attendant I met on a turnaround. She had transferred from New York to Orlando and seemed to be doing fine. "Traded Times Square Mickey for the real thing," she said.

Marlena was pretty, maybe forty, with chin-length bobbed blonde hair and blue eyes. The company likes this look and encourages it. They send hairdressers to the training center and to bases, where they subliminally try to convince us that blonde and bobbed is the way to go. At first I fought it, but soon I started hitting the peroxide. By the time I met Marlena, my hair was nearly white-blonde, although it was still too long and had to be pulled back in a ponytail.

"You have such petite features," one company hairdresser, Phil, told me. "A nice bob would take the years off. It would make your cheekbones pop."

Phil was blonde, with yellow highlights. His hair stood up in gelled spikes. He looked like an albino porcupine.

Marlena's hair was cut beautifully. It swept down in a perfect arch and made a J-curve around her jaw. I was sure Phil had nothing to do with it.

On the jumpseat, waiting for takeoff, Marlena and I chatted. Flight attendants have a ritual called jumpseat therapy. We meet each other, prep the flight, then plop on our jumpseats and tell the stories of our lives in precisely the time it takes for the plane to get off or on the ground. I don't know why we do this, but we all do. Maybe it's the design of a jumpseat, bodies pushed together, thighs and hips and shoulders touching, physical intimacy giving over to other kinds. Or maybe there's comfort in knowing that outside any given flight, we remain strangers and aren't likely to run into each other any time soon. Or maybe it's just the nature of the business, the lack of connections on the ground. Maybe it's the same impulse that leads drunks to talk to strangers about their bowel habits.

Whatever it is, there are flight attendants all over the company who know my failed dreams, and I know intimate details about people whose names, even now, I can't remember. But I remember Marlena.

We were on the jumpseat and I was asking her what brand of blonde — store or salon, Garnier or Clairol. I wanted to know where she got her hair done. I told her I needed a change.

She smiled in an odd way and said, "I go to Bumble. I spend a fortune to keep this thing up. It has to be exactly right, you see."

She pushed back the hair from her forehead and right cheek to show me the scar. It was jagged and brown and looked like an artery that had been ripped open. The edges were serrated and the skin around the scar toward her hairline was lumpy and looked bruised. Marlena held her hair back like that for what felt like a long time. I wanted to look away. Anywhere else, looking away would have been the right thing to do, but on a jumpseat, things are different.

"It's been a year," she said.

She'd been living on the Upper East Side, a good neighborhood, expensive, no rats or roaches, a good building, a brownstone, four stories, no doorman. She was coming home from a Vegas all-nighter, around five in the morning, exhausted. She didn't see the man, didn't know where he came from, until his pushed through the security door as she dragged her bag behind her. He started hitting. He beat her so badly the police asked if she knew him because they didn't usually see this much violence in rapes by strangers. He had a razor. He cut her face. He told her he was going to cut her face off. He would have killed her, probably, if she hadn't started screaming and kept screaming.

The police, when they came, told her she was screaming fire fire, just like they teach you in Girl Scouts, but she didn't remember doing that. The police caught the guy. There was a trial, a conviction. She had operations.

"I just came back on the line last month," she said. "The company flew me down to Atlanta to meet with a group of supervisors before they'd let me come back. They said it was to see how I was doing. They really wanted to see how I looked. Can't go scaring the customers."

She let her hair fall back into place and smiled and everything was perfect again.

The great writer Raymond Carver once said he was a cigarette with a writer attached. Brendan Behan, the Irish playwright and poet, called himself a drunk with a writing problem. Me, I was a pair of wings with a notebook I never talked about.

I should have told Marlena this. I should have told her that I knew, even then, that someday I'd write her story down. I should have told her why. I would have liked to have said something to her other than "I'm sorry," other than "Christ." I would have liked to have said something comforting, whether Marlena needed it or not.

*   *   *

"Last call for Hotlanta, woot woot!" Gary's voice prances down the jetway, annoying as feedback. I store the woman's bag over her seat, 3B, First Class. I hand her the standard mite-infested blanket and pillow, and make a show of fluffing the latter until it is almost three-dimensional.

"You airplane people are so sweet," she says, and puts one doll-hand in mine. It's strange, not because she touches me, but because she insists on making eye contact before she lets go.

The woman is nice, too nice to be traveling in First Class. Some flight attendants choose to work First Class because they believe it adds status to the job. They believe First Class passengers are more civilized than Coach passengers. It's not true, of course. This is just something working-class people think about people with money.

But this woman does not ask for an omelet or lobster. She doesn't want a fuss. She is polite. She says thank you. And on top of all that, because my parents are old and awkward travelers, I'm soft on her.

Still that bag is ridiculous. My back already aches and I have a twelve-hour day ahead. What could have been so important that this miniature woman tried to carry a bag that could carry her?

It was Gary's fault of course. He should have checked it.

*   *   *

One of Gary's other favorite jokes when he does check passengers' bags goes like this: "You know what our airline name stands for? Don't Expect Your Luggage to Arrive." Then he sends the passengers on board, where they panic in the galley and press their faces to the cabin-door window and try to spot the ground crew putting their bags in the belly of the plane.

Hotlanta. Gary's word for the great capital of the South.

Jagoff. Pittsburgh's word for people like Gary.

"Jag? Like Jaguar?" Gary says. "That's one sweet ride."

*   *   *

I scan the manifest and find the woman's name. Mrs. Clemons. I bring Mrs. Clemons orange juice and a biscuit.

"Thank you so much," she says. "I don't like to be trouble. It's my son, you see. He makes me fly up here. My son, he worries. I have arthritis and the bigger seats, well, he says it's better. My feet don't swell up as much if I've got some moving room. I don't like to be fussed over, though. I'm okay sitting in back. I tell him, 'I'm fine.' But ever since he's been in that band, he gets me these tickets and he says 'Mama, you fly First Class; First Class for my mama.' What can you do?

"My son, he plays horn. You like music?"

I nod. She is wearing me down and this time when I smile, I mean it.

"My son, he just loves playing horn. I always say, you have to find what you love in this world. Take you, for instance. You must love what you do, being so nice to help me and all. It's a blessing, Lord, it really is. A blessing."

I want to tell Mrs. Clemons I don't believe my job is any kind of blessing. But she seems so happy to talk about her son and it feels peaceful to listen. All around us call lights go off like game-show buzzers and people scowl and check their watches, but I pretend not to notice. For now, there's only me and Mrs. Clemons and this, I realize, is making me feel better. Not good, but better.

Some days, I like disappearing. Other days, there's comfort in being seen. I've given away free drinks, champagne, headphones—all the perks we are supposed to reserve for when we spill hot coffee or run out of meals or live through rough air—just because someone asked me how my day was going and waited for an answer.

This is why I wrap up a bottle of red for Mrs. Clemons. I'm sure she doesn't drink. She might even take offense, but it's the best I have to offer, along with some chocolates.

"Oh, you shouldn't do this. You shouldn't fuss," she says. "But thank you. I don't know if it will fit in my bag, though. Gracious."

She laughs and pats me on the arm. "I'm going to tell my son how nice you've been. He worries, my son. He plays horn, like I said. I never much cared for rock n' roll myself, but it's been a blessing, really it has. He plays with this nice man, Bruce Springsteen. He's from New Jersey. You know him?"

* * *

Clarence Clemons. The Big Man. Mr. C. The Reverend C.C.

In concert, Springsteen liked to tell about the time the Big Man joined the band. It was, he says, an event of near-biblical proportions that night Clarence Clemons showed up during a storm and opened the door to the Student Prince Club where Springsteen was playing for fifteen dollars a week on the boardwalk in Asbury Park.

The wind, Springsteen says, just blew the door off the hinges and Clarence stood there, lightning and thunder at his back and said, "I'd like to sit in." They played "Spirit in the Night." Midway through the song, their eyes connected. And that, Springsteen always said, was that.

Clarence Clemons. Tiny Mrs. Thelma Clemons's son. All six-foot-three, 300 pounds of him.

*　　*　　*

The Christmas after I meet Mrs. Clemons, The *St. Petersburg Times* will run a story, "An Angel Named Clarence." The story will be about Clarence's volunteer work with Jesus And You, or JAY, a crack-house-turned-mission on Avenue S in Riviera Beach.

In the story, Clarence and the mission's founder, Brother Bob Felder, will sit at a long table with residents and listen to their stories. Henry Mason Jr. will talk about the time he was shot in the stomach and came to JAY to heal so he could kill the man who shot him. "But instead," Mason will say, "I healed my spirit and feel like I have a purpose in life now."

Jennifer Clayton will say she used to be a hooker and a coke addict and JAY helped her regain custody of her five children. Bill Clark, who'd spent most of his 47 years in prison, will touch Clarence's hand. He will say, "I used to listen to this man's music when I was sitting in prison. This is something beyond my wildest dreams."

ROUGH AIR

Clarence will tell the reporter, Dave Scheiber, that he learned all about kindness and love from his parents, who were sometimes too poor to buy anything but comic books for their children for Christmas. He will say, "It only takes one person, a person to treat the problems from the inside out."

Scheiber will call the mission a place "where many lives have been pulled back from the brink and rejuvenated." He will say Clarence Clemons made broken lives wonderful.

* * *

When our flight is over, I help Mrs. Clemons with her bag. I walk her to the end of the jetway. I thank her for flying Delta and wish her a good day and hand her off to a gate agent who is not Gary. Everything is the way it always is, and I doubt Mrs. Clemons will remember me after this flight. I'm sure she tells her stories to every flight attendant she meets. I'm sure she is always open and unassuming and that she never thinks about it. But on this flight today, she may have just saved my life. I would like to tell her that. Mrs. Thelma Clemons, who taught her son everything about kindness.

You'll Love the Way We Fly

I'm in the galley making coffee. I try to look busy, not in the mood to talk or help.

This is the fourth leg of a six-leg day, and already I'm tired. I immerse myself in counting and recounting stacks of plastic cups, tightening the handles on metal coffee pots, scrubbing the steel galley counter until I can see my face, distorted and greenish in the plane's fluorescent light, eyes flecked with dried mascara.

I hear him coming before I can see him, the rustle of his nylon bag brushing against seat backs, the heads of other passengers. He is old, thin. He plops the bag on the floor of the emergency exit row, right across from where I'm standing. I'm engrossed now in stocking Cokes into the beverage cart. I watch him from behind the galley wall, a talent all flight attendants learn, covert ways to size people up.

His hair is gray, and saliva has settled into the corners of his mouth. He holds a filthy handkerchief to his nose. He is coughing, a deep-lunged cough, the kind that fades into a feathery wheeze then begins again, a terrifying, endless loop. A pack of Marlboros is tucked into his left sock.

I am afraid to go near him, afraid of what I might catch. When you make your living on an airplane, there are things you become afraid of, like germs and crashes and how cold the ocean is off LaGuardia in winter.

"They're not supposed to let them on like this," says my friend, who's working with me. They're not supposed to let them on drunk, either, but this is how it is. This is what I think, but I don't say anything.

The man coughs, then follows with his wet-rattled breaths. I think—this is serious, maybe not contagious, but serious. I call to him from the galley. "Sir, would you like water?"

He wheezes, coughs, shakes his head. I look at my friend, who's busy alphabetizing magazines and stacking pillows in the overhead bins.

"Excuse me, sir?" I say. "Can I get you something?"

He coughs, points. Coffee.

"Cream and sugar?"

He nods and so I bring him what he wants, along with some water.

"Thank you," he says, and grabs hold of my hand. I feel myself pull back. His hand is damp and cold, the fingers are all bone. "Thank you, I—." He coughs again, and I don't get the rest, so I have to lean closer— "really appreciate."

Later he tries to give me a tip. Two quarters wrapped in a wet dollar and held together with a rubber band. I say "no, no," but he presses it into my palm, gasps "You take it for taking care. I appreciate."

The effort of breathing has made him sound foreign. He's American, I'm sure, a New Yorker, though disease has taken the hardness out of his eyes. They are brown and damp, the whites yellowing like old paper. Still, he thinks small kindnesses are things you have to pay for.

I haven't really been kind. I've just done my job, against what I wanted, despite my own disgust. I am paid to smile, to talk to strangers about the latest issue of *People* magazine, to bring coffee and water, to make people comfortable.

I take the money.

"What is it you say?" he's asking, but I don't understand. "What is it you say on TV?"

"You'll love the way we fly," my friend sing-songs from the galley.

The man nods gravely, repeats it.

I laugh now. I don't know what else to do. He's dying, I'm sure. Emphysema or lung cancer, probably, like my father.

The flight is only an hour, D.C. to New York. When the man gets up to leave, I keep my head down, eyes focused on my hand, checking off items on a list. What we need: tea bags, stir sticks, band-aids, first aid cream, two bags peanuts. I try not to think, but I can't help it.

Who will be there in the airport to meet him? What is his home like?

Who brings him coffee the way he likes it?

Who is not afraid to touch him?

Sexy NYC

Today it's a cane-fight between two senior citizens on a JFK/Ft. Lauderdale run. One guy wants his seat reclined. The other guy wants his tray-table space. First guy pulls out the cane he stored under his seat. He threatens to whack the other guy over the head. Other guy climbs over his seatmates to get to his own cane in the overhead. Next thing, it's something out of *Star Wars*, except with canes.

The call lights go off. People point. They tug my flammable blue polyester blazer, poke my thighs and ass, whatever they can reach.

"Do something," one woman says, and I do.

I grab one of the canes. I block the other cane with my shoulder. This sends one guy toppling into the lap of a lady in a fancy velour pantsuit. Her Bloody Mary and pretzels go flying. She demands a free round-trip ticket and free dry cleaning. She threatens to sue, which makes the first cane-guy threaten to sue, and the other cane-guy threaten to sue, demand a free ticket and an upgrade to first class, where he says he'll try to forget about this by drinking as much free champagne as he can.

I hate my life.

I came to New York to be a writer. Instead I'm a flight attendant. I want to be done with it.

"No more," I say to the men and wiggle my pointer finger. "No more."

They both hate me. It's the one thing they agree on.

I took this flight attendant job so I could be based in New York. Now I don't write. I have a tiny rent-controlled apartment in Queens and I'm never home. I don't have furniture. I don't buy milk. I keep my toothbrush in the fridge so cockroaches won't crawl all over it. I sleep on a sofa bed that came with the apartment. The sofa bed never stretches all the way out, so I sleep in a V. It takes me a while to stand up in the mornings.

"You must revise your life," the great writer William Stafford used to say.

I'm trying. I've been sending out resumes for publishing jobs, editing jobs, anything that has something to do with words. When I checked my voicemail earlier, there was a message, a lady who wanted to set up an interview. She left a phone number, an address — 350 Fifth Avenue.

"The Empire State Building," she said.

And now I think my life is going to change.

For the rest of this horrible flight, I imagine taking the E train to the 6 every morning. I'll stop at a corner deli for coffee in an "I Heart New York" cup. I'll take the elevator to my office in one of the world's most romantic buildings, a building so legendary I never thought of it as functioning office space but more of a movie set, the kind of place where ordinary people can be transformed. *King Kong, An Affair to Remember, Sleepless in Seattle.* The great ape, Cary Grant, Meg Ryan and me.

More call lights go off. I ignore them.

"A person could die on here and they wouldn't even care," the woman in 28 B says. She's wearing a surgical mask. She thinks the ice that airlines use in drinks is poison.

On the ground, I call about the job. I call from the free phones in the flight attendant lounge. "Thursday, yes," I say.

I cup my hand over my mouth, try for privacy. All around me, other flight attendants are calling home, hands cupped to mouths, or they're collapsed on recliners, alarm clocks in hand, drooling into neck pillows, waiting for their next flight out.

It doesn't matter that I can't remember which job I'd applied for, which company the woman on the phone represents. She beams through the phone like an emergency exit.

"One thing," she says before we hang up. "How do you feel about adult content?"

"Not a problem," I say.

* * *

Before all this flight attendant business, back in grad school, I was the editor of a literary magazine. We'd done special issues against censorship, and published a terrible poet named Antler who wrote a lot about fellatio and hemorrhoids and being naked in the wild.

"He's our Whitman," one of my grad-school poetry professors said. I thought of myself as open-minded, progressive. I think of myself as open-minded, progressive. I tell the woman on the phone this. I don't ask what she means by adult content.

On Thursday, I take my trains. I stop at a deli, buy a coffee, a sesame bagel, a *Daily News*. I like living out my own New York story. I imagine my life as a script by Woody Allen, who says in *Annie Hall* that a relationship is like a shark, it has to move forward or it dies. I love that line. Here I am, moving forward. Here I am, not dead.

I'm early, so I hang around the lobby, take in the art deco and avoid the security guards. I don't want to look like a tourist in this building full of tourists. With their communal air, their somber clothes, most Manhattanites are beautiful accessories — tiny diamond studs, a silk scarf, a pair of Louboutins — worn by the city itself. I've worn my one black suit. I don't have the budget or ankles for Louboutins. I had to look up the pronunciation of Louboutins (LO-BOO-TANS). I shined my flight attendant shoes and they look okay, but I worry that everything about me blares desperation.

I check my reflection in anything that shows it. Everything shows it. Walls, windows, a steel beam. I pick and prod my hair, which I've swept up in a twist, and check my teeth for sesame seeds and lipstick. At one forty-five, I find the elevators that will take me to my new life. I check my reflection in those, too.

When the doors slide open, I enter a narrow hall lined with Mapplethorpe prints — huge lilies, an image of a man's naked and muscular back. This, I think, is a good sign. I know some things about Mapplethorpe. I know Jesse Helms, that censorship nut who spent most of his life in the senate, hated Mapplethorpe and began a campaign against the NEA because he felt the government shouldn't support "vulgarity." I could talk endlessly about Helms in my interview.

There is only one door at the end of the hall, so I open it. The receptionist, her burgundy hair pulled and waxed into a high ponytail, has a phone balanced between her ear and shoulder as she goes on typing. She's a marvel of multi-tasking, because she can still wave at me with her chin. I can tell from the chin point that I should sit, so I do, in one of two plastic chairs against the far wall. The room is tiny, run-down. There are no magazines to read, nothing to distract. The chairs face the receptionist, so I stare at her like she's on TV.

When she finally hangs up, she says, "You must be our two o'clock. Kathy will be out shortly."

I smile, nod, nod more. The receptionist smiles back, crooked, the kind of smile people sometimes give to lunatics, then goes back to typing.

At 2:30, Kathy comes for me. She is a large woman. She wears a man's tie and suspenders with cartoon figures on them—little Porky Pigs and Bugs Bunnies dance over her breasts and wide shoulders. I think she's going for a pop-culture Charlie Chaplin look. I think she must have a porkpie hat hanging on the back of her office door.

"Sorry you've been waiting," she says. Her voice is throaty and warm. "Come on back."

Kathy leads me through a tight maze of cubicles and a few more Mapplethorpes, then into her office. Her desk is piled high with paper. Her computer is decorated with animals made from pom-poms and attached to the top and sides of the screen by sticky, oversized human-y feet.

"So, you're a writer," Kathy says. "Looking for editorial work, correct?" She leans back in her chair and it squeaks. She tucks her hands under her suspenders, the way detectives do on TV.

There is one window in Kathy's office. From it I can see New York stretched out, all possibility. "Yes, yes," I say. "That's right." I lean forward. I want to look eager. I probably look like I've just been tazed.

"Your background is impressive. The position I have open, though, is entry level," Kathy says. She lets the suspenders go with a snap.

I mutter something about wanting to learn, paying my dues. I want to say as long as no one here tries to beat each other with canes, as long as no one here hands me a leaky diaper or sends me on a layover in Cleveland, we're good.

Kathy says, "And I mentioned the issue of adult content?"

"No problem," I say, and compliment the Mapplethorpes.

Kathy says, "So you could work on something like this?"

She opens the top drawer of her desk and pulls out three magazines. She fans them in front of me. The names, blasted in bold, are simple, direct—*Sexy NYC; Legs, Legs, Legs;* and *Suck Me.*

I try not to let anything register.

"Sure," I say.

I don't touch the magazines. I don't move at all.

Kathy says, "You might want to take a look at them to get a feel for what we do." She pushes the magazines closer. I pick one up and leaf to the centerfold. A woman in a black fishnet crotchless bodysuit is bent over, back to the camera, her wrists bicycle-chained to her ankles. Her ankles teeter on see-through Cinderella stilettos. The woman's face is mostly obscured, but her long dark hair hangs down onto the floor. The floor looks wet, industrial.

"That's a good one," Kathy says. "It's part of a photo essay we shot in the meatpacking district. We do a lot of photo essays."

I have nothing against porn. I learned a lot about sex in college from *Hustler.* I've rented porno flicks and learned to give head while watching *Flashpants* at a drive-in in the 80s. I like erotica. I think The Rabbit vibrator is genius engineering. I've enjoyed Amsterdam's red-light district. But I wasn't expecting that all my New York dreams would one day rest on working for a magazine called *Suck Me.*

It's a lot to take in.

"What you'd be doing mostly is writing captions," Kathy is saying. "Do you think that's something you'd be interested in doing?"

I nod and for a moment, believe it. And then Kathy hands me a take-home assignment. It's a series of caption-less black-and-white photocopied pictures. In the first picture, a woman in large glasses and a lab coat is holding an empty test tube. As the series moves along, she loses the lab coat, the glasses, her hairpins, her regulation nursing shoes and so on. For some reason, she holds on to the test tube, even in the last spread-eagle shot.

I feel my writer-neurons click on despite everything — *Why the test tube? What's the story here? Where are we going with this? Is this lab woman a sympathetic character? What does this all mean?*

"No more," I'd said to the old men on the plane, but there's always more.

Hope is built on more. The idea of more is, most days, the only way to go on.

"Just take this home, write the captions, then fax it back to me by tomorrow," Kathy is saying.

My reverie crumples. Fax it. Fax it where?

Tomorrow, if everything is on schedule, I'll land in Kansas City at 10 p.m. I imagine walking into an all-night Kinko's, in Kansas — Kansas! — and handing over my project to a clerk who will remind me of my sixth-grade music teacher. I imagine trying to fax it from the flight-attendant lounge where a southern Barbie of a supervisor will creep up, tap me with her fake French-manicured nails, and say, "We don't ah-prove of such thangs hare at our airline."

I look out Kathy's window. From up here, there are no sounds of the city. New York might as well be nothing but a postcard.

I thank Kathy and put the photos in my bag.

"You might want to take these along," Kathy says, "for inspiration." She winks, then picks up the magazines and hands them to me.

"Of course," I say, and grab at the magazines. I stuff them in my bag.

I thank her for the opportunity. I back toward the door. I let myself out through the maze of Mapplethorpes, down the elevators, out into the street where I nearly knock over a hot-peanut cart.

I walk block after block and feel sick.

I think about Kansas City. I think about a stop-over in Little Rock. I think about the beverage cart, the trash cart. I think about all those call lights lighting up into their own kind of city. The magazines in my bag are more promising than that. At least I'll be writing. At least I'll be here, in New York, on the ground.

Being grounded as a kid is a punishment. Being grounded now is a dream.

On my way to the subway, I try to feel better by stopping by the library to check out some Whitman and Ginsberg, those huge voices. Now there are two New York writers who, if they wrote what people called porn, did it on their own. I plan to take Whitman and Ginsberg home to my empty apartment. I plan to open a bottle of wine that a pilot friend brought from a Paris run. I plan to get drunk and weepy and then write my captions for Kathy, who might very well hire me and save me from Kansas City now and forever amen.

I check out the books and head for the exit. As I pass through the theft detectors, a guard—a huge grim-faced man who looks like George Foreman before George Foreman sold grills—touches my arm.

"Miss," he says. "Open your bag."

I stand there. I watch his lips. His teeth look like Scrabble tiles. I think about faking bad Spanish. *No hablo ingles.*

"Miss," he says again. "Your bag."

He points. I stare at his arm, all those meaty muscles. I think of all the things he must have seen. This is New York City, after all. People must have come through with stolen books, at least, or better, body parts, a brain floating in a mayonnaise jar, an eyeball in a cup. A guy on my last shuttle flight to D.C. snuck a Chihuahua through security and got caught because he'd tucked the dog in a zippered pocket of his jacket and run it through the x-ray belt. Some savvy TSA agent spotted the skeleton, all those wriggling bones.

The magazines in my bag are not stolen. They are not a body. They feel like a body, what's left of my own gouged-out heart.

Whitman sang the body electric.

Whitman said, "I exist as I am and that is enough."

Whitman said it is lucky to die.

I unzip my bag.

There, on top, is my complimentary copy of *Suck Me.* On the cover is an image of a man, eyes closed, his face content as a baby at a breast, running his tongue between the toes of a perfectly pedicured foot, the little seashell nails tipped red, the ivory ankle cocked in delight, and, above it all, a woman's disembodied fingers dangling a pair of strappy spike-heeled red sandals that are, I'm sure of it, Louboutins.

PART 3

The author at 17, playing piano
in her parents' living room.

Maybe Nobody's Born Anything

My bio-brother says his father was in the movie business. He says his father played piano. His father, my bio-brother says, was an amazing piano player, long fingers, a real natural.

Bio is what my brother and I sometimes call each other to make sense of things. It's hard to find language for what we are and how we feel about it, so sometimes we don't bother at all.

I am forty by the time my brother and I meet. He is a few years younger. When we're together, he and I like to compare hands. We press our palms together, measuring. Our hands are big, long-fingered.

"We get it from the old man," my brother says.

*   *   *

My brother and I weren't raised together. His mother gave me up for adoption before he was born. His father abandoned his family for Hollywood years ago.

My brother's mother is my birth mother, but when I say mother and father, meaning the parents who raised me, I say "real."

When my brother says mother, he means the mother who raised him, a woman I've never met. When my brother says father, he means a stranger.

*   *   *

My brother asks if I play piano.

I tell him I do.
He says he hopes I'll play for him sometime.
I tell him I will.

*   *   *

Soon my brother and I will be together in my basement and I will play songs on the piano I learned on as a child. The piano is over 30 years old, an upright Kimball, but the keys are good. My mother, the mother who raised me, kept the wood polished with oil soap, so it still shines.

I do my best to keep it up.

I polish it when I can.

I play my brother "Begin the Beguine," my father's favorite song. My father, the father who raised me, was a singer, before the war, before the mills, before he got bitter and sad and stopped singing.

Once he won a contest and got to sing on the radio in Braddock, Pennsylvania, and for a while everybody knew him as "the boy who sang on the radio."

Then they forgot what song it was he sang.

Then they forgot it was he who sang it.

Then they forgot my father's name and how to spell it.

Then they forgot my father ever sang at all.

The song he sang was "Begin the Beguine." The story goes, my father cut a record that day as part of his prize, but I never saw a record. No one did. My father must have kept it hidden or destroyed it.

Or maybe there never was a record. Maybe that was just a story. Maybe there was just that one time in the radio studio, one take, the DJ picking his fingernails, saying, "This is it, kid. You got five minutes."

My father always thought the song's title was "Begin the Begin," as if any minute his life would start over, as if any minute it would be good.

I tell my brother this and laugh, even though I think it's sad.

It's one of the saddest stories I know.

*   *   *

I play my brother another song—"Somewhere My Love," my mother's favorite, the theme song from *Dr. Zhivago*, a sap story set in the Bolshevik Revolution.

I have always hated this song.

My mother would make me play it over and over for guests.

I tell my brother this story, too.

I tell him about the time my mother made me play it for her cousins, Dick and Stella.

"Dick was a bastard," I say.

"I know a lot of bastards," my brother says. "You know what I mean," and puts a hand up for me, a bastard, to high-five.

*   *   *

I'm 16 and Dick and Stella have just pulled up in their paneled station wagon. They're staying for the weekend. I hear Dick say, "Jesus fucking Christ," and I hear Stella apologize three ways.

I'm hiding out in my room when I hear my mother call, "Oh Lori baby. Come say hi to Dick and Stella. Come play 'Somewhere My Love' for us." It's her singsong, welcome-to-my-perfect-home voice.

My mother watches a lot of old movies. She's spent a lot of money on me—piano lessons, dance lessons, doctors, clothes and food. What she wants every once in a while is to impress people—in this case Dick and Stella. What she wants is for me to come out and be, just once, a perfect daughter. What she wants is a lacey white dress and pigtails and for me to say, "Oh yes, Mother dear."

What she wants is for me is to curtsy and skip.

Most times I try. We keep our fights between us. In front of other people, I want her to be proud of me. I love my mother. I want to prove I haven't been a complete waste.

With Dick and Stella, though, there's a problem. Dick is nasty. He's also a drunk. He beats Stella. I do not know how often or how bad, but she is always nervous and he is always rough, and everyone in the family knows this and no one says much about it.

"You know how men are," the aunts say.

"They have a lot of passion between them," the aunts say.

"Dick has an artistic temperament," the aunts say, that word again, temperament.

I think Dick's name suits him. I tell my mother this.

"You will be respectful," my mother said before Dick and Stella arrived. "They're family," she said, as if that explained anything.

By artistic, the aunts mean Dick is a musician, a barroom pianist, and a good one. When he plays, Stella sings along, like the terrified little lab mouse she is.

Dick is not trained, like me. He reminds me of this each time we see each other.

Trained pianists, Dick says, are like trained monkeys. "Real musicians don't have to be taught how to run a scale or play the blues any more than real monkeys have to be taught to swing from trees and fling shit."

"You're either born with it or you're not. Me, I never had one goddamn lesson," he says now as he settles into my mother's good wing-backed chair.

He's wearing Hawaiian shorts and a tank top, black socks and sandals, even though it's October, even though there's frost coming. He has a can of Iron City in one hand. The other hand keeps time to some music only he can hear.

I think Dick is like a dog in this way. He's always hearing things.

He taps out those rhythms on the arm of the chair. He rolls the beat through his fingers, like they're already on the keyboard, like they never can rest. I watch his fingers, how thick they are, how big and hard his hands seem.

I imagine him hitting poor Stella, those fingers coming down again and again in a slap. I can't imagine what she'd do that would make him so mad.

"My sweet Dick," she says, and her voice warbles and clicks, like a cotton candy machine filled with pennies. "He plays like an angel."

Maybe it's something awful and simple.

Dick the angel-playing pianist can't bear the sound of his wife's voice.

"I'm a natural," he's saying. "I play by ear. Have since I was this high," Dick says, and he takes his rhythm hand down low, an inch above the carpet, to show he's been playing since he was a fetus.

*   *   *

Stella's tweaking, a Pekinese on the 4th of July. When Dick tells her to get up to the piano, when he tells her to sing along to what I am about to play, she jumps like an M-80 just went off in her shoe.

Poor Stella with the horrible voice sings when Dick says sing, even if he'll slap her for it later.

I play my best for my mother, who wants to be proud, who wants to show me off, her well-trained and talented daughter. My mother sings along with Stella. They smile at each other as they sing. They hold hands, like singers do in those movies they watch.

The two of them could torture dictators into giving up their countries, their families, their stashes of fine cigars, their own ears, they're so beautifully unimaginably off-key.

When it's over, Dick just sits in his chair.

"Well, aren't you two the bee's knees," he says to my mother and Stella. He doesn't smile. His fingers thrum their invisible keys. He's quiet, then he says to me, "I can see you've practiced that one a lot."

I nod and think for a minute he's going to praise me.

He says, "You've been taking lessons for how long — three, four years now?"

He says, "How about I give it a go?"

He hoists himself out of the chair and walks to the piano like a linebacker. He sits down on the bench and it creaks under his weight. He rolls one wrist to loosen it, then the other.

Then he plays.

I'd like to say he's terrible. I'd like to say he hits the keys with a jazzy rendition of chopsticks. I'd like to say he thumps the keys like the brute he is.

But he plays beautifully. His fingers don't even seem to touch the keys. His whole body becomes part of the instrument, the music. There's no separating it.

Dick is a beautiful pianist and the world is worse because of it.

"There," he says when he is finished. "That's how a piano's meant to be played."

Weeks later, I'll get a letter from Dick, who will tell me I have the technical skill to be a concert pianist, but not the heart. I have the physical ability, but not the soul. I should give up and not waste any more time.

"I figure I should tell you now for your own good," he says. "You are not a born pianist."

It's a crushing thing.

"You'll thank me," Dick writes.

*　　　*　　　*

I didn't thank him that day. I didn't thank him ever. I wished him dead more than once. I wished Stella would kill him in his sleep — a pillow to the face, a stove left on, something easy like that.

Still Dick was right. I wouldn't become a pianist, though all these years later I still play, and one day I find myself sitting in the basement of my childhood home, playing the piano Dick once played, the very same piano, for a man who is my brother.

"You're really good," my brother says. "Just like my old man."

Maybe I wasn't born a pianist.

Maybe nobody's born anything, though Dick thought he was.

"I know a lot of dicks," my brother will say. "My father was one most of the time."

I won't know if my brother's father is my birthfather.

I won't be sure if it matters or not.

"Do you know any Bruce?" my brother will ask, and he'll mean Springsteen.

THERE IS NO DUST IN MY HOUSE:
ON WRITING ABOUT MYSELF AND OTHER PEOPLE

Years ago when I was a young journalist, my editor put me on The Love Story beat. My job was to interview people about how they fell in love, then churn out sentimental stories their friends and relatives could laminate and stick on their refrigerators.

"Happy crap," my editor, a spine-y displaced New Yorker, called it.

One pair of blind professional bowlers aside, most of the interviews I did were forgettable. Except one—a sweet old couple married over 50 years.

He was a World War II veteran. She stayed home, raised their kids and volunteered at the church bingo. These were Norman Rockwell's people.

"Ad fodder," my editor would say. "Schlocky copy."

The couple invited me to their house. They were sweet and funny, open and kind. Their house was full of family photos and antiques, afghans and doilies. The man swore and his wife said, "Lord, this man." They gave me tea. They gave me sugar cookies from a fancy tin. I went back and wrote the story. My editor ran a big picture of the two of them holding hands. I felt good about it.

The day the story ran, I got a call in the newsroom. It was the wife. She was screaming and I had to pull the phone back. I tried to figure out what I'd done to make her so angry. I'd printed that her husband swore? I didn't know.

Turns out, there was a line in the story where I described their living room. I'd written: "In a room filled with family photos and dusty antiques."

"I can't go to church," the woman screamed. "I can't go to card club. You've ruined me."

She said, "There is no dust in my house."

I was 22 years old.

I didn't know dust meant anything.

I tried to figure out how to run a correction, how to make the woman feel better. "There is no dust in Mrs. X's house. The Times regrets the error."

But there was dust.

But maybe I didn't have to mention it.

*   *   *

"There's you and me, and there are other people," the poet Bei Dao once said, a warning against both a writer's self-indulgence and carelessness with other people's stories.

What to leave in, what to leave out. It's always a question for writers. It's a question of both heart and craft, and it's especially a problem when the subject is another living person, when the subject is someone else's life.

In her essay "What the Little Old Ladies Feel," about how she came to write her memoir *Fun Home*, Alison Bechdel wrote, "No matter how responsible you try to be in writing about another person, there's something inherently hostile in the act."

In that same essay, Bechdel refers to Faulkner's famous line: "The writer's only responsibility is to his art. … If a writer has to rob his mother, he will not hesitate; the 'Ode on a Grecian Urn' is worth any number of old ladies."

I believe Bei Dao. I believe Bechdel and Faulkner. What they say about writing, about writers, is true for me, too. But how, as a writer of memoir, as a writer who deals in true stories, can I navigate that?

"I want peace and grace and beauty," the great Studs Terkel used to say. "But how do I get that?"

Three memoirs in, I still don't know.

*   *   *

In 2004, I started an adoption search. My daughter was born with a birth defect I'd been born with, and I realized, with the startling clarity that comes with any emergency, that I had no medical history to offer my children.

I was also grieving. My mother died less than a year before, my father five years before that. Through my search, I was trying to get more than a medical history. I was trying to replace the parents I lost. I was trying to find a way around grief.

It's as irrational as it sounds. I didn't know that then. I was navigating by desperation. I was navigating by hope.

Some facts about my adoption search:

I never got a medical history. My dead parents stayed dead and the emptiness I felt from that never changed. My experience with my birth mother was not the happy reunion people see on TV. Still, I connected with members of my birth family and became close to one of my brothers.

There's more to the story — which I detail in my third memoir *Belief Is Its Own Kind of Truth, Maybe* — but those facts are a start.

At the time we met, my brother knew I was a writer. He'd read my first book and then my second. He liked the books and passed them to friends and relatives as evidence of something.

That I wasn't a crackhead, maybe.

That books made me respectable, like a coffee table.

That a writer was someone who could be trusted.

"It wasn't like you were just some nutball off the street," he said.

There's a fable, about an alligator who promises to ferry a mouse to the other side of a swamp. The mouse makes the alligator promise not to eat him. The alligator promises. The mouse gets on the alligator's back and rides across the swamp. Once they're on the other side, the alligator chomps down. "What did you expect?" the alligator said.

"A man must live according to his nature." Thoreau said that.

To know your own true nature, to accept that, is a good and terrible thing.

*   *   *

When we first met over wings and beers, my brother said, "You have to promise me you won't ever write about this," and I said, "I can't promise that, but I promise to give you a heads-up if I do."

I knew even then I would write about it. I don't think it would have been possible for me not to do so. Writing is my nature. I write when I'm confused, when the world doesn't make sense and when I'd like it to line up a little. I write to figure out what I think and feel. I write to discover something true about myself and the world and my place in it. I write to connect with other people who might be confused and lost like me. I write about myself. I write about other people.

I write about other people.

And so of course I wrote about my search and other things, too — motherhood, what it means to be a mother, what it means to be someone's child, what people do to one another in the name of family.

Maybe at some point, drunk or sad, I promised my brother something else. I don't remember it that way, but he does.

*   *   *

I finished the manuscript that became a book 10 years after my brother and I first met. It took me that long to find a shape for my story, to figure out what my adoption search might mean and why I hoped other people might care about it a bit.

In 2014, after I'd gotten a contract for my book, I started talking with my brother about it.

"So there's this book I've been working on," I said. "I want you to read it. I think you need to read it."

What I didn't say was, "I want your blessing."

What I didn't say was, "I want you to be okay with this."

What I didn't say was, "Forgive me."

His response, over and over, was the same.

He said he didn't need to read it. It was fine.

"Do what makes you you," he said.

He said, "I'm okay with whatever."

He said, "Go Steelers!", his way to get around talking about anything else.

I knew it wouldn't be that simple.

I wanted to believe it would be that simple.

*   *   *

When my book came out in August, I gave my brother a copy and asked him again to read it. I asked for forgiveness, and this time I said it. There was, I knew, no taking anything back.

I didn't want to take anything back. I wanted my brother to understand that silence wasn't an option. I wanted him to understand that I needed — for reasons I didn't understand until I did — to write this book.

An adopted person is always someone else's secret. I was tired of secrets most of all.

My brother didn't understand.

He didn't understand why I'd reveal secrets, even ones that, to me, weren't secrets but facts I'd taken from my own redacted adoption records. Adoptees' records are called Non-Identifying Reports.

He wanted to know why I wrote about things I wasn't entitled to write about.

That's the word he used, "entitled."

As someone who works in a university, I hear the word "entitlement" batted around a lot. I hadn't thought about it in relationship to adoption before, the distinction between a right and a birthright. I hadn't thought about it in relationship to being a writer, either.

What stories am I entitled to tell and what stories are off limits? What story do I, as a person without a legitimate history, have a right to tell?

*   *   *

If there is dust in a house, does a writer mention the dust or not?

It depends on whether the dust matters and how much. It depends on what dust has to do with a bigger truth.

"Write one true sentence," Hemingway said. "And then write another one."

The truth always hurts someone, I think.

*   *   *

"I thought I could write about my family without hurting anyone, but I was wrong," Alison Bechdel wrote. "I probably will do it again."

Then she wrote a follow-up memoir to *Fun Home*. It's called *Are You My Mother?*

*   *   *

"You own everything that happened to you. Tell your stories," another writer, Anne Lamott, says. "If people wanted you to write warmly about them, they should have behaved better."

*   *   *

My brother didn't understand why I'd reveal family secrets, but for me, the word family is loaded. If I were to draw a line around family, it would circle my husband, my children, my dead parents and me.

When I say my friends are family, I believe that in spirit, but it's not true.

When I say my brother is family, I believe that in spirit, but it's not true. We are not family in the traditional sense. We were not raised together. We don't have the same loyalties, the same secrets.

When my brother said, "we're family," there was a subtext of *omerta*.

Family means pact.

Family means, "We don't talk about things."

Family means staying on the surface.

Instead of talking about family, we say other things. "Go Steelers," my brother would say.

* * *

I don't know if family will come to mean silence for me one day.

I don't know if, when my children are older, I'll ever ask them not to speak of things.

I hope not. But already when my son or daughter remembers something that doesn't match my memory of it, I find myself correcting things.

"It wasn't like that," I say.

I say, "Here's how it really was."

I say, "You're remembering wrong."

* * *

I wrote about other family members in my book, too—members of my adopted family, extended family, my father and mother, my husband and children.

Each story, each moment I wrote I considered carefully in revision. I asked, "Do I need this?"

"I take only what I need." This is what I believe so I can live with myself, doing what I do.

Did I need to mention dust in that love story years ago? Probably not.

Did I need to tell the truth about my adoption story? Did I need to include everything I included?

I've thought about that a lot.

Yes. I do, I did.

And I would do it again, and probably will.

There's a very real cost to telling that kind of truth.

My brother and I haven't spoken lately.

It's something I'm learning to accept.

miss new york
has everything

Lori Jakiela

"Wonderfully comedic,
beautifully written,
honest, sad, wise—
*Miss New York Has
Everything* truly
does have everything
you look for in a
great memoir."
—JONATHAN AMES,
author of
Wake Up, Sir!

There She Is, Your Ideal

Outside Sam's Club there's a bubble machine, like on Lawrence Welk. It's meant to be festive because this is a grand opening, a new store on the outskirts of Pittsburgh, but customers swat the bubbles like flies. A creepy clown with a button that says "Free Hugs" chokes balloons into poodles while a woman with a Marge Simpson up-do hands out free-hotdog coupons like she's doling dollars from her own wallet. A teenager with boxers that poof from his jeans like a life preserver shows people where to get the free cake.

"Keep a song in your heart," Lawrence Welk, that polka pimp, that purveyor of wonderful, said so often it's on his tombstone.

I'm trying.

*   *   *

When my publisher's in-house publicist Annie called to say she'd set up a book signing for me at Sam's Club, she said, "Don't snark. It's a good opportunity." She said, "It's not just any Sam's. It's a Grand Opening." She said, "Sam's moves a lot of books." She said, "Sedaris does Costco all the time."

I know I should be grateful. Years later, I'll realize how grateful. But for now, this is my first book and with each day its failure, my failure, becomes more obvious and heart-sinking.

For every writer, the first-book dream is different. For me, it was a review in *The New York Times*, maybe

O Magazine. It was NPR with Terry Gross, who'd teach me to sound sexy-serious and let me touch her hairdo because we'd be instant friends like that.

What's happened, though, is pretty much nothing. I check my pulse-less Amazon sales rankings every 15 minutes, even in bed under the covers. I Google myself. I Google myself again. I Google myself again and my husband swats me because he wants to sleep.

"Just write another book," he says, but there's this one to hope for and mourn first.

*   *   *

Annie the publicist is perky as an Alka Seltzer, but I know and she knows my book isn't selling enough to make back my advance, which is death for my writing career. Lately I've been doing what I can. I've been giving readings at dive bars and senior citizen centers, in basement book clubs and at 4H fairs.

Last week I gave a reading at a club where people were armed with Nerf guns and threatened to shoot if they didn't like what they heard. I was prouder than I should have been when they didn't shoot.

Sam's Club, by most accounts, is a step up from a Nerf assault, but it's depressing like all things Walmart. A few years back, some kids from my high school alma-mater started the website "People of Walmart." It's supposed to be funny, but it usually makes me sad, even when the pictures are of a guy banana-shopping in a red Speedo or someone's therapy goat munching flammable lingerie. It's depressing to think of everything in bulk, all those florescent lights and security cameras, smiley cartoon faces rolling fair-wages all the way back to China.

It's depressing to think how often I end up shopping there.

"Of course I'm in!" I told Annie about the signing, and made my voice match hers bubble-for-bubble.

I hate myself.

*   *   *

Today I got dressed in my writer outfit, all black—black dress, black tights, black kitten heels, black scarf. It's a fancy get-up, as fancy as I get, but the dress is worn and pilling at the sleeves and armpits. It used to fit perfectly but now it pulls across hips that never got back to their pre-baby size. No matter what I do I look tired. I *am* tired.

My daughter Phelan is almost two. She wakes off and on all night. My son Locklin is five and wakes early. I'm not sure how much sleep I get but it's not a lot. My husband Dave trims my hair with his electric razor, because these days I don't have time or money for a real haircut. If I tilt my head, my hair looks almost even. I convince myself the ragged ends make me look edgy. I pass my dark roots off as punk.

"Thanks for doing this for the family," Dave says, about everything, and I say it back to him.

Even in the mornings, my breath smelling like dead dog, dark circles under my eyes like a boxer's, he calls me beautiful. I love him, and I believe he loves me, but he's a writer, too, and between love and children and jobs and writing and bills and laundry and trash day, the world is exhausting us both.

Today I put on more makeup than usual. I squeezed into two pairs of Spanx until my stomach looked almost flat. I checked my dress for spots—milk, spit, toothpaste, a soggy Cherrios smear. I filled in a bleach stain with black Sharpie.

When I left, Dave was on the floor playing Star Wars with Locklin.

"Be him," Locklin said, and passed Dave a toy Yoda.

Dave ran Yoda up the hem of my dress. "Fuck you I would," he said.

"He can hear you," I said, and cocked my chin toward Locklin, who was oblivious, deep in a light-saber battle with Luke Skywalker.

My husband swears so much and so often no one notices he swears.

I bent down and kissed them both on the tops of their heads.

"Good luck," Dave said, and I said, "Seriously. It's Sam's Club."

"Get some toilet paper," Dave said. "We're low."

*   *   *

At the Sam's Club entrance, I ask the teenager in charge of cake for help. "I'm here for a reading and book signing?" I say. "Do you know where I should go?"

"A book on signing?" he says. "Like sign language?."

He throws up a peace sign, then says, "There's free cake inside to the right," and juts his chin to show the way.

I don't know much sign language, but my favorite sign goes like this:

Put your left forearm flat in front.

Take the first two fingers on your right hand and make a peace sign.

Turn your hand upside down.

Pretend the fingers are legs.

Stand the legs on your left forearm.

Consider the forearm a bridge.

Send the little person you've made diving off the forearm, legs kicking.

Make a silent screaming "O" with your mouth.

It's how I feel.

*   *   *

Inside Sam's Club, everything — the signs, the cake, the carts, more Grand Opening balloons — is red white and blue, as if Sam's is America itself and not just a place where Americans get a bargain on 1000-count boxes of latex exam gloves.

People ram by, massive carts stuffed with paper towels and dog-food bags big enough to stash bodies in. Behind me a woman in a motorized scooter with a red balloon tied to the back revs up. She says, "Beep," extending the vowels into a screech. She waves her arms like propellers. "I'm trying to get through here," she says. "Jesus Christ."

I make my way to the information desk. I've brought a copy of my book and hold it up to show the woman at the desk. She's wearing a regulation Sam's vest. It's covered with American flag pins, smiley faces, and buttons that say, "Ask Me! I Can Help!"

I say, "I'm here for a book signing? Do you know where I'm supposed to go?"

"A what?" she says.

"I'm an author," I say and point to my book. "I'm supposed to sign some books here?"

"I don't know nothing about that," the woman says and holds up a finger, then reaches for a big red phone that looks like a cartoon.

Off toward the snack bar, the giant free cake seems mauled by squirrels. The line for free hotdogs stretches back to the entrance. The 300-count bags of roasted pig-ear dog treats are buy-one-get-one, which explains why nearly every cart that rolls by is stocked with them.

*   *   *

My book, by the way, is called *Miss New York Has Everything*, a line I took from an episode of the 1960s TV show "That Girl." In the episode, Marlo Thomas, an independent woman making her way in the big city, enters the Miss New York pageant. As part of the competition, she makes a cheesecake with all New York ingredients. Things go, expectedly, wrong.

I thought the title would be ironic, maybe, but most readers thought it was Chick Lit. When I'm around other writers, to say the title of my book makes me wince.

"Don't worry," my agent said. "Men aren't your audience anyway."

The cover of my book features bubble print and a picture of a smiling flight attendant. The top of the flight attendant's head is cut off. The cover and the title don't reveal much about what's inside — mostly a story about growing up in a mill town, Trafford, PA, then moving to New York to be a writer and becoming a flight attendant instead, then moving back home.

If I saw my own book on a shelf, I wouldn't buy it. I'd think it was about shopping for Louboutins. I'd think it was "Sex in the City."

"I want not only to be loved but also told I am loved," the Victorian novelist George Eliot said.

George Eliot's real name was Mary Anne Evans. She took a man's name because she didn't want to be dismissed as a woman writer, which meant either a romance novelist or a hysteric.

George Eliot was smart, but not beautiful. Her family made sure she was educated as backup. Not a good candidate for marriage, she became a writer instead.

*　　*　　*

The information desk woman seems to be on hold. I'm trying to do math—how many roasted-pig-ear dog treats can an average American household get through in a year—when I see the sign. It's behind a wall of stacked toilet paper. The sign is huge, like something from a used-car lot, yellow bulbs forming a giant flashing arrow. The arrow points to a spot behind the toilet-paper wall.

On the sign, a message in bold black letters reads: COME MEET LORI JAKIELA. All caps. There's more, but the toilet-paper wall blocks it out.

"That's me," I say to the woman on the red phone. I point to the sign. "It's okay I'm her."

The woman looks doubtful. Then she says, "Whatever you say," and keeps the phone to her ear.

I turn and walk toward the sign. My name is there, in lights, even if they are used-car lights, even if these lights flash behind mounds of very reasonably priced toilet paper, even if the lights are smack in the center of a giant conglomerate where the air smells like old hotdog water. I feel pretty good.

"I want not only to be loved but also told I am loved," George Eliot said and she didn't mean herself just as a woman, I think. She meant as a writer. She meant her books.

I look around again at all the Sam's Club shoppers, all those readers and book lovers, and realize I have been a ridiculous neurotic ungrateful malcontent. I promise to call Annie the publicist first thing and apologize for being the jerk I am.

"My life is going to change," a character from one of my favorite Raymond Carver stories says. "I feel it."

He means, of course, it isn't, but I'm not considering that.

*   *   *

As I get closer to the sign, I notice a long line of mostly middle-aged men, waiting. My agent said men weren't my audience, but here is evidence. I feel myself filling up with myself, like a Grand Opening balloon, all pride and hot air.

I walk past, smiling, waving.

I say, "Hey there." I say, "Nice to see you." I say, "Thanks for coming."

Nearly all of the men wear Dockers and polo shirts, various blues and beiges. Some of them have cell phones latched to their belts. There's a lot of cologne. Like the woman at the information desk, the men seem confused. Some check their watches, waiting for the real show to start.

When I get to the front, I see why. There's the full sign, which close-up is so bright it's blinding. The rest of its message, the part that had been hidden by toilet paper, reads:

COME MEET LORI JAKIELA
MISS AMERICA

I stop in front of the sign. I step back. I look at it. I squint. I look again. I will it to say something else. I think maybe there are two of us here, me and Miss America. I think it's a grammatical error, a missing "and," a lost comma.

Then I think, no.

Annie talks so fast, she's so perky, it would be an easy mix-up. Miss New York. Miss America. I stand in front of the sign for what feels like a long time. I look down at my dress, the blacked-in bleach spot, my un-shined, un-beautiful shoes. Six months ago, I would at least have had my post-preggo boobs, but now, nothing.

Off to my right, there's a long table. Annie was right about one thing. Sam's has ordered a lot of books. Stacks of them are piled up, ready for Miss America to sign, bubble hearts dotting all her i's.

A chair rests at the table. A small placard in front of it repeats my name, my alleged title, in case the flashing car-lot sign isn't enough.

I walk over. I sit down.

*   *   *

The questions start at once. The first guy in line, who may have been here an hour or more, bends down to look under the table, like I might be hiding someone else underneath there. His hair is gelled. It doesn't move when he bobs down and up, twice. He reaches in his back pocket and pulls out a picture of himself with, I think, the most recent Miss America.

He says, "You are not her."

He says, "I know her."

He says, "This is false advertising."

His face is red. Above his upturned polo collar, a vein pops in his neck like a worm. He stomps a foot. "I'm getting the manager over here now," he says.

He starts to walk away, then turns back. He leans over and puts both hands on the table in front of me, like he's a lawyer on TV. He's wearing a school ring. It's tight and his finger poufs out around it like a sausage. I stare at his finger because I don't want to look at his face. I wish both of us invisible, gone.

He says, "And when exactly were you Miss New York?"

It goes on like this. Some of the men wander out of line. Others want to vent. One asks me to stand up so he can see my legs. At first I don't know why, then I realize he wants to compare them to the flight attendant's legs on the cover of my book.

"Those aren't even your legs," he says, loud and over his shoulder so the others can hear.

He's right. Those are not my legs. My legs, underneath the black tights I'm wearing, are mottled and bruised. When we took the kids on vacation to a kiddie water park, my husband noticed all the other parents there looked a lot like us — everyone bruised and swollen, lumpy and exhausted. It was easy to sort the parents from the non-parents, like we're two different tribes.

"The world is beating the shit out of us," my husband said. "All the parents look like crack whores."

To the man in front of me, I say, "It's a stock photo," and laugh a little. I say, "She's probably not even real."

The man glares at me, like I've tried to sell him swampland, like I've denied him his slice of free cake.

I say, gentler. "I'm not on the book, but I wrote it."

I think this should count for something.

I hope it will count for something.

*   *   *

"You must love your work and not be always looking over the edge of it," George Eliot said. "You must not be ashamed of your work and think it would be more honorable to you to be doing something else."

George Eliot, whose great intellect trumped beauty, went on to have steamy love affairs and eventually married a man 20 years younger than her. In portraits, she had lovely blue eyes.

I won't think of George Eliot until later, of course. For now, at this table, it's just this man and me. He picks up a copy of my book, the book that took me a lifetime to write, the book I thought would change everything. He turns it over like he's checking nutritional value on a cereal box. Then he tosses it down.

"All lies, I bet," he says.

"Miss New York," he says. "Some joke."

*　　　*　　　*

When the manager comes over, he's sweating. He's been fielding complaints. He says, "Well, it's nice to meet you I guess." As he's talking, he turns the placard in front of me face down. The manager also wears Dockers and a polo shirt, the uniform of his tribe. His hair is smoothed into the beginning of a comb-over. He looks at the flashing sign. He says, "There's not much we can do about that, other than unplug it," which he does. He doesn't apologize. He offers me a free hotdog, some cake. He says, "You're supposed to be here two hours, but I understand if you don't stay that long."

"Oh. that's okay," I say, and try to come off as congenial, Miss Congeniality, a consolation prize.

"Sam's moves a lot of books," Annie had said.

I stay the whole time. I'm not sure why, other than there are all these books and I feel like I should stay with them, the way a captain is supposed to stay with a sinking ship. I take out my notebook and start writing. I take a lot of notes. This makes me feel better, like the words are righting things.

*   *   *

A woman, who may or may not be the same one who beeped at me earlier, whizzes up in her electric cart, the red balloon still bobbing behind her like a buoy.

"What is that, a catalogue?" she says. "What are you people selling now?" Then she revs off, rams a toilet paper tower, and sends a massive pack flying.

Another woman in a matching leopard-print stretch top and pants stops by to say she was a Pennsylvania Junior Miss back in the 1970s.

"I was for real," she says.

No one buys a book. I don't sign a single copy. In the moments between visits from people who want to talk or shout at me, I look at the image of the woman on my book cover, her full red lips, wide smile, perfect legs. Under the table, I curl my legs back and think of the witch's legs disappearing beneath her house in *The Wizard of Oz*.

"Fuck you I would," my beautiful husband said to me on my way out the door.

Still. I touch my hair. I wish I'd brought lipstick. I wish myself beautiful or invisible, both.

*   *   *

When my two hours are up, I grab my copy of my book. It's ragged, dog-eared, marked up from the readings I've been doing. There's a chocolate-milk sippy-cup stain on the back.

The manager comes over to say goodbye. "I think we moved some inventory, so it wasn't all for nothing," he said.

He said, "Did you get a hotdog?"

*   *   *

At the Sam's Club exit, a security guard stops me.

"I'm going to need to see a receipt," the woman says.

"I didn't buy anything," I say. "I'm an author. I was here for a book signing."

The woman points to my book. She says, "I need to see your receipt for that," she says.

I point back over my shoulder to the sign. I point to my name on the cover. My name is in bubble print next to the flight attendant's perfect left calf. I say, "That's me. I'm a writer. This is my book."

"I'm going to need to see some ID," the woman says and doesn't smile.

*   *   *

George Eliot said, "It's never too late to be what you might have been."

George Eliot said it first, but people have forgotten that. Now her words are everywhere, on refrigerator magnets and t-shirts.

You can buy them in bulk.

You can get a good deal.

The Plain Unmarked Box Arrived

The night we ordered the sex chair, we'd been drinking. Not a lot, but enough to make a sex chair seem like an investment, like junk bonds or an IRA.

The kids were asleep. My husband Dave and I were at the kitchen table, recovering from our son Locklin's 7th birthday. We'd thought we'd kept it simple—bowling party, pizza, cake.

"We'll go easy this year," I'd said. "Low stress."

Last year, we'd had a party at home. We hired two clowns, a husband-and-wife team named Spangles and Spanky who ran ads in the *Pennysaver*. They were a bargain—$200 cash for two hours, including a magic show, a live animal show, face painting and balloons. I felt lucky to find them. But minutes after they arrived in a rusted-out Chevy van smelling like smoke and stale beer, we knew. The clowns weren't happily married. They were late, according to Spangles, because Spanky couldn't follow directions to save his checkered ass. Spangles, according to Spanky, could go straight to hell. They argued in our driveway. Spangles kicked Spanky with her huge clown feet. Spanky waved a lit cigarette close to Spangles' rubber nose and flammable face paint. Later they let a goose and a terrier loose in our basement, made the birthday boy wear a toilet seat as a lei, fashioned a pair of balloon boobs, and set off firecrackers on our new rug.

"I don't care," Dave said when the subject of Locklin's birthday came up this year. "No more clowns."

So Lokay Lanes it was. Lokay Lanes — the local bowling alley where, 10 years ago, the Farrelly brothers filmed the movie *King Pin*.

The only line I remember from *King Pin* is this one, from Roy Munson (Woody Harrelson), a dethroned champion bowler with a rubber hand — "The world can really kick your ass. I only have a vague recollection of when it wasn't kickin' mine."

Not much had changed at Lokay since the Farrelly brothers first visited — same neon lights, same beery-carpet smell, same nice people spraying the same rental shoes with Lysol.

Earlier that day, it had been Dave and me and 19 sugar-rushed first graders. We tried to keep them from knocking each other unconscious with bowling balls. They tried to show how strong they were by picking up heavy things, usually me. Our three-year-old daughter Phelan tried to stuff cake into the automated ball returns. About 20 minutes in, the kids realized that all the toys in the party bags — glow sticks, lollipop rings, gummy wristbands — could be used as weapons.

Once, years ago, in a judgment lapse that was probably a psychotic break, I'd dated a Special Forces guy. He used to hold up things, like dental floss and empty toilet paper rolls, and say, "You know I could kill you with this if I wanted to."

You'd think I would have learned, but no.

It didn't help that Locklin's party had an army theme. The cake was shaped like a soldier in full combat gear. The boys fought over who got to eat the head.

"I call brains," one buzz-cut kid who did gang signs during the group picture kept screaming. "I call brains."

There was a joke I used to tell the Special Forces guy. Why do you think they call you special?

"I feel like they're winning," Dave said when brains-boy stabbed him in the butt with a pink glowstick.

"They are," I said, and plucked icing out of my hair.

Back home, we were finally alone. We had beer and frosted mugs. We had Townes Van Zandt on the stereo, a frozen pizza in the oven, and a new copy of *Rolling Stone*. We sat across from one another, raised our glasses, and smiled. Dave was wearing Phelan's lime-green monster hat, a fuzzy number with bug-eyes and devil horns. It looked like a possessed condom on his head. My hat was a black newsboy. I thought it made me look like Izzy Stradlin, if Izzy Stradlin were a middle-aged suburban blonde woman who still giggled at lines like, "well, is he straddlin' or isn't he?"

I know. The sex chair. I'm getting to that.

But first, background.

This was the way we spent most Saturdays. We wore funny hats, played music that didn't call for hand claps or puppets, drank cold beer and stole time while fans whirred in the kids' rooms to block out noise. Not that we made much. We kept our voices down, the music turned low. Locklin would be furious if he knew we were awake and having fun without him. He hated to miss things. Before he went to bed every night, there were questions.

"So," he'd say, his eyes like two coin slots. Seven years old and already sure everyone was trying to get over on him. "Staying upstairs all night?"

A few years back, we'd finished the basement and built two offices — one for Dave, one for me. One night, Locklin woke up scared and went to find us. We were both downstairs, each in our own little office. Locklin was incensed. Downstairs was too far away for us to save him from things like vampires and owls and boredom. Also, he couldn't hear what we were up to.

"Absolutely, we'll be upstairs," I'd say.

"Oh yeah?" he'd say. "What are you going to do?"

"Nothing much," I'd say. "Take a bath. Go to bed. The usual."

"You need sleep," he'd say.

"I love you," I'd say, and start to back my way out.

"Love you too," he'd yell and pull the covers over his head. He'd pretend to snore, but I knew he'd never go down that easy.

Lately, it had gotten worse. The slightest noise set Locklin off. He'd come stumbling blind down the hall, half naked, angry, sure he'd been tricked into sleeping through the best moments of his life. These days, if Dave and I wanted to have sex, we had to wait until morning, when Locklin was off at school. Phelan slept late, and so we had an hour there, before work. If we wanted to have sex at night, we had to sneak, latch the bedroom door, keep the bed squeaks to a minimum, and listen for footsteps, a jiggled doorknob, the sound of small covert breathing.

Which is why the sex chair was doomed.

It started as a joke. Dave found the ad in *Rolling Stone*. There was a website. A few beers in, and we were inside the world of The Liberator dot com. We were flirty, having fun, putting the day and all its small humiliations behind us. We joked about the shapes of vibrators, the seriousness of the dominatrix models, the practicality of glass dildos and six-inch stiletto boots. Then we wandered over to the furniture section.

"New waves to groove," the front page read. "Put some funk into function."

The furniture looked like it came from Barbie's Country Camper—overstuffed swooshes in everything from earth tones to zebra prints. When not in use, each piece converted to a chaise that promised to "Cradle all the right places and recharge sexual energy."

Dave and I had been married for over seven years. We still had sexual energy, but it was that word—recharge—that was so appealing. Plus the furniture looked really comfortable. And it was on sale. For just under four hundred dollars, we could recharge. Revitalize. Reclaim.

"What do you think?" I said.

"It's a steal," Dave said.

I dug out the credit card we usually reserved for groceries and car repairs. Dave typed in the numbers.

Six days later, The Esse arrived. It was huge. The box was plain, unmarked. We had trouble getting it through the front door. All the pictures of The Liberator furniture had shown two beautiful people sprawled in a wide-open space, a loft probably, a bachelor pad straight out of *Esquire*. Mod art on the walls, wood floors covered with animal skins. There was no other furniture in the shot.

"Where are we going to put it?" I asked Dave when we finally got the Esse unpacked. We'd ordered it in navy blue. It matched the living room and our bedroom. The Esse wouldn't fit in either.

"Downstairs?" he said, and it seemed perfect. The basement, the side away from our offices, was a wide-open space. There was a fireplace. We'd painted the main room creamy beige, the same color you see in coffeeshops. The color was soothing, sensual. And most

THE PLAIN UNMARKED BOX ARRIVED

of all, the space was private, a whole floor down from the kids, though of course we'd have to be careful. We'd have to plan. This made it exciting.

"Wear thigh highs," Dave whispered while I scraped dried egg off the dishes. I made a note to dig my lingerie out from my sock drawer

"If you go to Sheetz," I whispered as he played Mr. Potato Head with Phelan, "Don't forget batteries."

But then Locklin came home from school, and went, oddly, straight downstairs. He usually stayed in the living room or went to his bedroom to play with his army guys, but not this time. Who knows why. It took him a minute.

"Hey, mom," he yelled. "Thanks for the cool chair."

I was horrified. The chair had lived up to the ads. It looked almost normal. Funky, oddly shaped, but it did blend in. If you didn't know what it was.

When I went downstairs, Locklin was straddling the Esse. A battery of little plastic army guys was lined up along the curves, like an invading force on a ridge. He was holding one of the bigger army guys and making gunshot noises and yelling "Let's go let's go" and "Look out!" and "Aaaarrrgh!"

"He thinks it's his," I told Dave. "It's creepy."

"Don't think about it," he said. "And don't talk about it either."

That night, we put the kids to bed. Phelan went right down. Locklin did his drill.

"Staying upstairs all night?" he said.

"Of course," I said, and tried not to blink.

"Okay then," he said, and that was it. "Goodnight."

"I love you," I said, but he already had the covers over his head.

What can I say about parenthood and married love?

LORI JAKIELA

All around my son's room, little plastic army men take aim. Sometimes it all feels like a battle between what we love and what we love.

"Nice to see you," Dave says on Saturday nights.

"Nice to see you," I say, as if we haven't seen each other in years.

Sometimes I think about Spangles and Spanky. It's not every day two clowns throw down in your driveway — the matching rainbow afro wigs bobbing, their smiles huge and painted on. Maybe they were just having a bad day. Maybe they're mostly happy. Maybe, when they take off the makeup and flashing suspenders, when they're just themselves, people with real names like Bob or Alice, they say, "Nice to see you," and fall in love all over again.

As for Dave and me, I found the thigh highs. I lit candles and the basement flickered like a movie set. Dave kissed me, and together we curled down into the Esse's soft, perfect curves. And then there were footsteps. Back and forth over our heads. Frantic.

"Mom?" Locklin called from the top of the stairs. "Dad?"

What can I say?

We left the chair in its place for a few weeks. Then, when Dave's parents came in for a visit, we hid it under the stairs.

"I don't think they'll know what it is," Dave said. "But just in case."

At first Locklin missed the chair, but now I think he's forgotten. Which is fine, because his father and I haven't. It's still there, under the stairs, waiting.

The Esse comes with an extended warranty. It's solidly built, real quality stuff. An investment, made to last through almost anything.

P.S.: Clarifications and Corrections in Regards to Previous Essay Entitled "The Plain Unmarked Box Arrived"

a) When I say we'd been drinking but not a lot, we were drinking a lot. That essay was originally published in *The New York Times*. If you write in *The New York Times* that you've been drinking a lot and also happen to be parents, you can expect the comments section to get ugly. Also it is unacceptable to talk about drinking in positive ways. If you do talk about drinking in positive ways, people assume you're hiding something and need to go into recovery. After an afternoon at the bowling alley, Dave and I needed recovery. We smelled like smoke and Lysol and feet. There was still icing in my hair. I found a Sour Patch kid in my bra. Dave was poked in both the butt and the eye with a glow stick. We think the eye shot was also courtesy of the kid who called brains. Think of how much booze it takes to wash that away. Double that.

b) Did I lessen the amount of drinking in that essay on purpose? Of course not, but I can see now that I wanted to impress *The New York Times*. If I impressed *The New York Times*, maybe *The New York Times* would introduce me to other sophisticated friends, and so on. Sophisticated friends do not take on new friends who have Kegorators in their kitchens.

c) The Kegorator was a Father's Day gift to Dave from me. I put the Kegorator on the credit card we used for groceries, car repairs, and a sex chair. It seemed practical. No more bottles. We were saving the planet. We were doing our part.

d) Dave and I know nothing of junk bonds and IRAs. We got married despite our lack of anything resembling financial security. Before we got married, we hocked the only bonds we ever had — gifts from Dave's grandfather for various birthdays and Christmases and graduations. The essay wasn't long enough for this to be explained. I apologize if I sounded financially-competent. We used the money from the bonds to buy our wedding rings and a couple Pick Two lunches from Panera. Dave complained about the size of his sandwich. My salad was okay. It could have used a few more olives.

e) We bought our wedding rings wholesale at The Clark Building. The Clark Building doubles as Pittsburgh's diamond district. It's not to be confused with the Clark Bar, a traditional Pittsburgh candy. A Clark Bar is flaky peanut brittle dunked in chocolate. A Clark Bar is delicious and affordable. The Clark Building is supposed to be a place where you can get a good deal, but who knows. Clark sold its Clark Bars to Necco in New England. Necco makes those wafers kids hate, you know the ones, a cross between fossilized Communion wafers and Tums.

f) The jeweler who sold us our rings had a watch that could double as a satellite dish. He had a porn-star mustache that popped when he frowned. The mustache looked like an expensive pet, something exotic and feral, a mink maybe.

g) Minks are ferocious and not tameable. They bite and are more or less weasels. Of all gemstones on earth, diamonds are the most common. A company named De Beers invented the idea that diamonds are both precious and forever, just like Coca-Cola invented the American idea of Santa Claus. Look it up.

h) It's easier to talk about minks or diamonds than it is to talk honestly about what matters—love and sex and family and time; how money and expectations, my own and other people's, can get in the way of all that.

i) "Every bride should shine a little," the jeweler said. Dave and I wanted two plain bands. The jeweler was trying to sell us on little diamond bits for my ring. I watched his mustache as he talked. It was hypnotizing. "You need a little sparkle for your special day," the jeweler said. He looked me over, my scuffed Doc Martens, my torn jeans, like I needed more shine than most. In the end, Dave and I threw down an extra $75 we couldn't afford for a few chips of diamond dust only we know are there. Dave was still paying off his DUI fines. The balance on my credit cards could have bought us a car that wouldn't break down.

j) When I said we'd go easy on our son's party, I used the phrase "low stress." Every party we threw for our kids has been high stress, mostly because of the cost. There was the clown party and the bounce-house party and the Chuck E. Cheese party where our son almost puked because Chuck E. Cheese, a giant rat with mange, was terrifying. There was the party at a place called Sea Base, which has a series of giant hamster tunnels kids get stuck in. You have to pay extra at Sea Base for kids to shoot each other in laser tag. I have more than once climbed into the giant hamster tunnel to set a kid free. It is expected that a parent, regardless of size or age, will crawl into the giant hamster tunnel to set a kid free when called upon to do so. It is socially unacceptable to avoid paying extra for kids to shoot each other in laser tag.

k) All the employees at Sea Base look dead inside, especially the one who gets stuck working the prize counter. The prize counter is where kids exchange vats of tickets for slap bracelets and stale candy and tiny plastic garbage cans filled with something called Toxic Slime. It will take the average kid 15 minutes to decide between a fistful of crusty Tootsie Rolls or a rubber sticky hand. It will take the average kid 15 minutes more of buyer's remorse to discover the sticky hand isn't sticky.

l) If we weighed our kids' parties against the $100,000 Tom Cruise threw down to celebrate his daughter Suri's second birthday with swarms of real butterflies and catering by Wolfgang Puck, we would be considered practical, reasonable. But even a low-rent kiddie party costs hundreds of dollars we didn't have.

m) "Can't we just have a cake at home?" Dave said, and I said, "And he can work that out in therapy later." When I say things like that, I sound like a mommy blogger. I sound like a TV sitcom. I sound like someone not myself.

n) A kid needs a party. I believe that. Dave and I have always disagreed on the definition of party. I felt like a terrible mother if I couldn't provide a party that resembled some of the neighborhood parties we'd been to recently. There was the party with the live pony rides and the party with the ladybug theme and the live ladybug gardens, and the party at the kiddie nightclub where the kids drank ginger ale out of champagne flutes and pretended they were at a rave and the DJ set off dance-floor smoke that smelled like hot chocolate. By neighborhood parties, I don't mean anyone living on my working-class street. I mean the people living in the big houses down the road in housing plans designed to sound regal—Deer Run, Lion's Run, Kings Manor, The Willows. The Willows has its own pond stocked with swans. A sign by the pond says "For residents only." A few miles up, there's one called Plantation Estates. One of the mansions there has a racist lawn jockey. Swans are mean-spirited and aggressive. I'd like to smash both the lawn jockey and a swan with a very fancy golf club. I do not golf.

o) Why would I try to be part of a culture I hate? My impulse to compete with parties thrown at the mansion-houses of my children's friends is the same impulse that led me to agree to the diamond-dust in my wedding ring. I feel bad about myself sometimes. "Why can't you be normal?" my mother said to me for years. I was adopted and didn't fit in. I didn't want to be normal. I wanted to be normal. It's a contradiction that stuck. "A kid has to have a proper party," I said to Dave, who rolled his eyes. "It's important to celebrate things," I said. "It's important to mark our children's milestones," I said. Please see mommy-blogger note above.

p) Lokay Lanes hasn't changed much since the 1970s. The bowling shoes are cracked leather. The laces are full of knots. The clerk behind the counter, in her blonde beehive, sprays everything with a huge can of Lysol, which explains the smell Dave and I were trying to drink off later. The carpet and the bowling balls are always sticky. "The kids love it there," I said, and Dave said, "The kids don't care. You do." "Bowling is fun," I said. "Don't ruin everything."

q) Note to self: when clowns take out an ad in the *Pennysaver* in the age of Twitter and Facebook, there's reason for concern.

r) "If he could fucking afford a cell phone, we'd at least have GPS," Spangles had said, and Spanky said, "Oh go to hell," and Spangles said, "I'm already there, buster," which is about when she kicked him with her clown foot. Bowling was better than that. Dave and I worry about paying our cell phone bill every month. Our cell phone bill is enough for a car payment. Two, maybe. Years ago, I was the one who wanted cell phones. I made a big deal about needing a phone to be safe.

s) I dated the Special Forces guy because he was a New Yorker and I was living in New York and was afraid to be alone there. He knew which subway to take. He knew when a cab driver was about to rip us off. Also I was broke and he fed me and helped with rent. I felt bad about it. All of it.

t) I married my husband for love, not money. We are not practical people.

u) Rose Castorini, the mother in the movie *Moonstruck*, asks her daughter, "Do you love him Loretta?" And Loretta says, "Aw Ma, I love him awful." And Rose says, "Oh God, that's too bad."

v) "You think everything's all daisies and roses," my mother used to say about love. "Wait. You'll see. Love isn't everything."

w) My mother wanted me to marry a New York stock-broker. She wanted me to go to the opera. She loved my husband and she wept when she was dying because she'd miss him so much.

x) My mother listened to Sam Cooke records. She listened to Perry Como, "My Funny Valentine." *Every day is Valentine's Day.* She fought with my father and once threw a glass milk bottle at his head. My parents fought over money. They fought over sex — my father wanted it, my mother did not. As a child, I should not have known this, but I did my share of sneaking around. My mother kissed my father's balding head while he slept. When she kissed him awake, it was on the cheek and she kicked a leg back, like something from one of those romantic movies she loved.

y) Dave and I used the credit card we reserved for groceries and car repairs to buy a sex chair because it's perfectly designed for things like 69 that would otherwise require acrobatics. Acrobatics make a lot of noise, especially when your bed is from Ikea and squeaks a lot. Squeaks are not ideal when your kids sleep across the hall. Dave and I used the credit card because the promise of time to have good sex without the worries that come with being parents was as important as paying our bills. It is as important as that still.

z) "Don't ruin everything," I said to my husband. I was speaking to the world.

CAGE MATCH

The scorpion's name is Cupcake, and Cupcake looks pissed.

"Oh come on," a zoo official with a walkie-talkie strapped to his waist says. "How scary can it be with a name like that?"

He's talking to a girl. The girl is on Cupcake's side of the safety rope. The zoo official is on the other.

It's the girl's job to pop Cupcake's carrying case open. Then she's supposed to reach in and scoop Cupcake like a gerbil.

From the way the girl is shaking, I'm sure it's her first time.

I should say, "Honey, are you crazy? Don't do that."

I should say, "Sweetheart, how much are they paying you?"

To the zoo official, who is about my age and still wears his baseball cap backwards, I should say, "Why don't you put your hand in there, dickhead?"

Instead I bring my 10-year-old son over to watch.

*　　*　　*

How I became this person, I don't know.

Earlier, I wanted to hang out at the shark tanks. Then on the rickety bridge over Otis the Alligator.

Zoos trigger something primal in me. Cute animals bore me. I'm interested only in animals that, if things were fair and cage-free, would kill me.

A zoo visit is about defying mortality, maybe. Most things are. It's something not to talk about, though, especially with my sensitive 10-year-old son, who worries the snow leopard is depressed, wonders if the octopus is lonely, and likes the penguin house most of all.

*   *   *

We were on our way to check out venomous snakes when I saw the Live Animal Demonstration sign.

How I justify watching:

I read somewhere that most scorpion stings are the same as bee stings.

I convince myself Cupcake is some sort of eunuch, a domesticated nub where a stinger used to be.

I think if someone's going through the trouble of picking up a scorpion the size of a Pop-Tart, the rest of us should pay attention.

"You've got to see this," I tell my son, who is a more decent person and who would rather not see this at all.

*   *   *

Cupcake's whole body is a claw. She's backed into the corner of her carrying case. Inside the reptile house, under ultraviolet light, Cupcake glows like a club kid at a rave. But out here, in the sunshine, she's so black she's almost purple, one oil-slick bruise. Her carrying case is pink plastic, the kind usually reserved for hermit crabs, starter pets. It's the kind of case kids store Barbie shoes in.

"Look, sweetie," I say to my son. "She's going to pick up that scorpion." I point, like I've just said something wise, a life lesson.

I've become the muscle-guy earlier back at the aquarium. He flexed, pointed to a tank and said, in a low and serious voice, "What we have right here are fish." His pretty girlfriend clung to a bicep and cooed.

My son doesn't coo. He backs up, because he's not an adult, because the world hasn't worn his heart to a nub, an overused eraser, because he still feels things.

"Why would she do that?" he wants to know.

The girl is ponytailed, in a powder-blue polo shirt with the zoo logo stitched on the chest. She looks like summer help, an intern, maybe. Maybe she's getting minimum wage. Maybe this is unpaid life experience and she's chalking up college credits she'll have to take out loans to cover.

"Because she's in training?" I say, and of course it comes out as a question.

"In training for what?" my son wants to know.

*　　　*　　　*

I've had a lot of awful jobs, terrible internships. "Life training," people called some of them.

None involved handling a scorpion, but still.

*　　　*　　　*

Once when I was a flight attendant, a pilot made me hold a door shut during take-off and landing.

There was a mechanical problem—the door wouldn't lock completely and the handle would start to open on ascent and descent. It was something that would normally ground the plane, but the pilot had a date in D.C. that night—one hot blonde, one strip-club steakhouse, jumbo margaritas served up in glasses shaped like boobs.

The pilot didn't want a delay.

He said, "Did you bring a parachute?"

He said, "You'll love the way you'll fly."

He said, "Come on, I'm joking."

He said, "Just don't let go," and winked.

I was young. I needed that job. I did what I was told. I pushed my whole weight against the handle and the handle pushed back. I don't know how dangerous it was really, but I could feel the cold air whistle around the door seal. The steel handle frosted and shook and any minute it seemed the door would burst and I'd jettison out, cartoon baggage, still strapped in my jumpseat and smiling.

I'd been taught to smile on the job no matter what. The door handle inched open and I smiled and the passengers kept calm. They looked at me like I knew what I was doing as I pretended to know what I was doing.

We went on like that until one guy started hitting his call button. He kept at it through the short flight. He was doing sign language to show he needed a drink, that he might choke and die if he did not get a drink, like this lack of drink was a noose stringing him up.

I smiled. He did not smile back. I shrugged and pointed my chin toward the seatbelt sign overhead, which demanded I stay seated, too—sorry, sorry—and that we'd both just have to hold on.

I held on.

He kept pressing his call light like a game show buzzer. The door stayed shut. By the time we were on the ground, I was shaking. There was a red imprint on my palm from the handle, and the man who wanted a drink was so angry he wrote down my name. He threatened to write a complaint even though I got him snacks and a diet Coke to go.

The pilot heard all of this but pretended not to.

"I think I can, I think I can," the pilot said as he pulled his pilot-cap low, gangster-style, and gathered up his flight bag.

"Nice work, little engine," he said, and patted my hip on his way out of the cockpit, off to his margarita-boobs and his blonde and the thick steak he liked juicy and medium-rare.

*   *   *

It's been a dozen years since I had a job like that, which is maybe one reason I can keep watching the girl and the scorpion now.

Empathy is an easy thing to lose, like car keys, like the name of that one actor in that movie about the scorpion king, you know the one.

*   *   *

"You can do it," the zoo official says as the girl loosens the clasp on Cupcake's case.

The zoo official claps his hands and tries to lead us all in a cheer.

You. Can. Do. It.

Boom boom boomboomboom.

*   *   *

"You forgot how to work," my father used to say, meaning me and what I do for a living now, pushing words around a page.

He meant, watch it.

He meant, first you're on one side of the glass, then the other.

He meant, don't be an asshole.

He meant, it's not work if it can't kill you.

*   *   *

At the entrance to the machine shop where my father worked for 30 years, a sign counted down the days since the last accident. The numbers were flip charts. It was someone's job to flip the numbers forward and back. I don't know whose. The numbers didn't go above two digits much.

My father had so many metal shavings in his skin. He said he set off metal detectors at airports. He never wore jewelry because it could catch in the machines at work and take a finger or worse.

"I want to keep all my fingers," he'd say, "so I can show the foreman how to stick it up his ass."

*   *   *

"I mean, seriously," the zoo official is saying, "Cupcake?"

It's a punchline he's sharing again and again.

It sounds cruel, mocking, but I don't think he means it that way.

Maybe he's walked people through this so many times he's lost count. Maybe he's forgotten what it's like to be young and afraid. Maybe he has kids of his own. If so, I don't think he'd want them to have this girl's job, but still. Maybe he works so much and is tired and can't think about that. Maybe he misses home and his kids. Maybe this girl and her hesitation are just more doors to push through.

Work kills people in many ways, I think.

*   *   *

When my son was first born, he cried all the time and no one in our house slept much. At first my husband and I thought it was colic, but it went on and on, and the pediatrician shrugged and said some children are born sensitive like that.

"He'll get used to it," the pediatrician said about my son and the world.

My husband worked a terrible corporate job back then. His boss, a linebacker of a woman who sucked diet Coke like air, would stretch an 8-hour day into a 15-hour one too often to count.

The boss liked to squeeze the plastic diet Coke bottles as she drank, as if the bottles were skulls she could crush in her fist. She promoted my husband to manager, which meant he was salaried, which meant, no matter how many hours he worked, there was no such thing as overtime.

His boss liked to quote politicians. "Pennsylvania is a right-to-work state," she'd say.

She liked to quote Dr. Phil. "You either get it or you don't," she'd say.

"Do not use your family as an excuse," she'd say when my husband said he needed to get home.

Once, after a stretch of six long days in a row, my husband came home, went into the kitchen, and took a serrated bread knife to his forehead. He carved. Blood ran into his eyebrows and down his cheeks. He came out and showed me. He was smiling.

"Genius, right?" he said, and I felt sick.

In the back bedroom, our son wailed in his crib. The train-car apartment felt like something from a funhouse, the narrow walls squeezing in. The ugly orange carpet felt damp, maybe seepage from the fridge that leaked and rattled and threatened to go out.

I thought about a friend who recently had a breakdown. "All I remember is being carried out of my apartment feet first," she said. "I was wearing these filthy pink fuzzy slippers. Hideous. I worried what people would think about my slippers."

I looked at my husband and wondered how I'd carry him out, down three narrow flights of stairs to the street, and who I could possibly call for help.

I said, "What the fuck are you doing?"

I said, "Jesus. No. Do not do that."

My husband, though, had a plan, not a breakdown. He called his boss and told her he'd been in a car accident and wouldn't be in to work the next day and maybe the next. He used the words "impact" and "head trauma," then hung up.

Pretty soon we were laughing. I cleaned his forehead with peroxide and we celebrated with drinks and take-out from an Italian restaurant nearby. Everything felt, for a moment, manageable. We remembered we were happy. We remembered we loved each other. Our son slept some. We did, too.

"Most men live lives of quiet desperation," Thoreau said.

*   *   *

"In training for what?" my son wanted to know about the girl.

"He'll get used to it," the pediatrician said about my son and the world.

*   *   *

The girl is shaking even more now, like she's about to stick a fork in a toaster. Cupcake's case is open. Inside, Cupcake flexes her tail, her very operational stinger. I look down at my son, who's squinted his eyes shut.

The girl tries to breathe. She cups her hand and lowers it into the case. She nudges it under Cupcake and brings the creature out, a heavy dark heart in her palm.

"Okay," she says to the zoo official who's beaming. "Now what?"

PART FOUR

The author's parents at the Copacabana Club, circa 1950s.

SHUT UP AND DANCE

I do a great Chicken Dance and a respectable Hokey Pokey unless I'm on roller skates. I polka, too, but it looks more like a seizure. At least that's what my father, Braddock-Pennsylvania born and working-class Polish, used to tell me.

"It's not like you're being electrocuted," he'd say. "Relax already."

In Braddock, there's a bridge — the George Westinghouse Bridge, a huge thing, a mountain of concrete stretching over Pittsburgh's Electric Valley. The Electric Valley is called the Electric Valley because George Westinghouse built an electric plant there.

Westinghouse saved many lives by giving people work. Laborers died building the bridge that honors him. Their bodies are still there, in the concrete.

Now, when Pittsburgh people decide to kill themselves, the Westinghouse Bridge is the bridge they often take. There's not much water underneath, mostly railroad tracks and rock. The backdrop is fire from U.S. Steel's Edgar Thompson Works, one of the few active steel mills in the Pittsburgh area.

"That's the bridge to take when things get serious," my mother would say. It was one of her favorite jokes.

"That's not funny," I'd say, and she'd say, "Says you."

My mother, like my father, was a beautiful dancer. I remember her at family weddings at Olympia Hall in the Electric Valley. My mother, all high heels and swirl,

LORI JAKIELA

backwards, forwards, never a missed step, and then my parents together, a pinwheel, more one person than two.

"Don't overthink it," my mother would say as she'd try to show me what she knew, but my brain and my feet would never cooperate.

"Monkey mind," Buddhists call it when thoughts won't hold still.

"Don't over think it," my mother would say about that, too.

Poor George Westinghouse. He wanted to do only good in this world. Then someone invented the electric chair and used his AC current to power it. Thomas Edison joked that dying in the electric chair should be dubbed "to be Westinghoused."

Thomas Edison was an asshole. Remember that.

Westinghouse built the town I live in and grew up in, the same town my mother lived in and grew up in, and her mother, and so forth.

Most people want to do only good in the world.

Most people want to be remembered for that.

I still visit my mother's grave on Mother's Day. We had a difficult relationship, my mother and I. Many daughters of fierce mothers will say the same thing. I loved my mother desperately. She loved me desperately, too. We didn't destroy each other. We came to some kind of peace before she died. That is its own kind of miracle.

But the loss I feel, her absence, is as palpable as her fingers on my pulse. As a nurse, she did that a lot. She'd check my pulse, my breathing, every vital sign. I never had a cold when I was young. I had upper respiratory infections. I did not have a belly button. I had an umbilicus. My mother's notes for school absences read like entries in the Physician Desk Reference.

Most kids think of the heart as love, something with a smiley face, not something physical, something mortal that can fail.

In second grade, my daughter brought a smiley heart home from school. It was a gift she'd made for me. The heart had paper accordion arms and legs. On the back, there was a message: "Mom you make my heart dance."

She was just then learning about the heart as an organ, something fleshy and beating inside her.

"Gross," she said, and held her hand to her chest. She pressed hard, as if she wanted to make it stop.

I want my daughter to live forever. I want my son to live forever. I want the hard world to bring them only joy.

"Don't overthink it," my mother would say.

I'm still a terrible dancer. My daughter, who loves Justin Bieber despite Justin Bieber, has tried to teach me to Dougie. We dance together in the kitchen, which was my mother's kitchen because we still live in Trafford, Westinghouse's town, in the house I grew up in.

"No, like this," my daughter says. She giggles when I can't get it right.

Sometimes my mother would dance alone in the kitchen, a little polka from the sink to the table on Sundays. That's when Pittsburgh radio stations would have Polka Hour and Frankie Yankovic would roll out a barrel of fun.

"Now isn't that happy music?" my mother would say.

The only dance I ever tried to teach my mother was the Hustle. I'm not sure I ever had that right, either, because I was very young in the 70s.

We'd dance to the Bee Gees, and Donna Summer's "I Will Survive."

"I don't take things for granted because everything feels more fragile," Bee Gee Robin Gibb said after the death of his brother Andy. "It's made me wonder about mortality and how long you've got somebody in the world."

What I remember about my mother: she was beautiful. I miss her.

"Shut up and dance," she'd say, "before the song's over already."

Begin the Begin

Cole Porter died over 50 years ago. I'm not a big Cole Porter fan, but his death gets to me because my father loved his songs.

"They're so cheesy," I'd say, and my father would say, "You wouldn't know class if it bit you on the ass."

My father's been dead for years, too. I've never stopped missing him.

People say time heals things but I've never found that to be true.

My father wanted to be a singer. He wanted to wear fancy suits like Cole Porter and stay in the luxury suite at the Ritz, but my father drove a beer truck, then he went to war on an aircraft carrier, World War II, off the coast of Japan. When he came back, my father said he didn't want to be a singer anymore. He came back as a mill worker, a machinist who worked in graphite, a practical thing.

"I'm not like you. I don't have time for pissing around," he'd say.

He'd fall asleep on the couch, head back, snoring like a dump truck. He liked cop shows, *Ironsides*, *Murder She Wrote*. He liked *JAG*, a show about a former Navy fighter pilot, a hero in a sharp white uniform, who turns good-guy lawyer. My father liked a hero. He liked lines that were clear — good guys, bad guys, justice as entertainment since he didn't see much justice in his life.

"You think this is a dream world you got another dream coming," he liked to say.

Time for me doesn't heal anything. It just makes things go deeper until everything echoes everything, until I can almost hear my father's voice when I'm stuck in traffic, stuck in a meeting, stuck.

"I don't know when I'll ever be old enough to stop being pissed off all the time," I told a friend the other day.

My father always sounded angrier than he was. When I told my father I wanted to be a writer, he was happy about it, I think. He paid my rent in college. He called me every week.

He said, "You never were good at math." He said, "How are you for money?" He said, "Are you eating good?"

He said, "Most people are cockroaches. Remember that."

He said, "Maybe there are one or two good ones."

He said, "Sweetheart, are you happy or what?"

My father was younger than me when he gave up singing. He was younger than me when he stopped believing in most people. I try to remember that, and all the unhappiness it brought him.

If he were here now, I'd like to give him a call and check in. I'd like to tell him I know the world is a shitty place, that lately lots of shitty things have happened to me and to so many people I love, that people hurt and go on hurting. But I'd like to tell him I know, too, that hope is the only way to work through some days. I'd like to tell him this because I need to remind myself of it. I'd like to say that even on the worst days, there's bound to be some small beautiful thing there and sometimes that's enough to keep going to the next day and so on.

Today I'd like to tell my father about the painted-lady butterflies my daughter's keeping in her room. She mail-ordered caterpillars—part of a science project she's doing for school—and together we watched them transform. There were six caterpillars. Five butterflies have hatched so far. The sixth chrysalis fell, so we followed the directions and nestled it on a napkin against the side of the butterfly cage. One of the other butterflies has been staying next to it since yesterday, keeping watch, maybe, worrying, who knows.

I like to think the chrysalis will open, despite the odds. I like to think later today my daughter will come home and she'll find six butterflies.

My father died before my daughter was born. My daughter could sing before she could say words. Her voice teacher says she has perfect pitch.

"Where did she learn to do that?" he says and I say, "Baby Mozart tapes?"

I tell my daughter she's like her grandfather. She asks if I think her grandfather would have liked her and I say, yes, very much.

Last night before she went to sleep, she said, "I think he's going to make it," meaning the butterfly of course, and I said, "I hope so."

If my father were here I'd like to tell him that hope, even if it's ridiculous, is a beautiful and comforting thing, like watching a butterfly learn to use its wings for the first time. Like putting a favorite song on replay.

When I think of my father, I put Mary Gauthier's song "Mercy Now" on and play it over and over. It's a good song. It's about what the title says, about how we all could use a little more mercy.

My father was a complicated man. I think Cole Porter, from the little I know about him, was complicated, too. All those bouncy musicals, all that sadness of his own split life.

When I was very young and people would ask me what my father did for a living, I'd say he was a machine. In the military, people are called property. When soldiers are hurt and other people are held responsible for it, the charges say "for damage of military property."

A few years out of the war, my father sang when he drank but then he stopped drinking. Then he'd sing only in church, so loud it embarrassed me as a child and I'd lean into my mother, like my father was some crazy person who'd followed us in, a stranger whose hand I didn't want to shake when it was time to offer the sign of peace.

My father was obsessed with Elvis, the way he played at being a soldier, the way he gave away cars, the way he took all the pills the Colonel gave him and died alone and was buried out back in Graceland by his swimming pool.

My father was obsessed with Sinatra, how in the end, after all his mob years, Sinatra was afraid to go to sleep, he was that afraid of death.

My father was disappointed when Johnny Cash cleaned up, fell in love with June Carter and lived. My father was happy, I think, that Cole Porter was, mostly, miserable.

My sad father latched onto other people's sadness like parachutes. Their disappointments, their failures, meant he wasn't falling alone. He loved Cole Porter's "Begin the Beguine" most and when I was very young, my father bought me the sheet music and asked me to learn to play it on the piano. It was the only song my father ever asked me to learn to play, so I did. For a while he'd want me to play it over and over. Then, for no reason I ever knew, he stopped asking me to play it.

Cole Porter wrote "Begin the Beguine" when he was drunk at the Paris Ritz. Later, when reporters asked him about it, he'd say, "I never can remember that song."

IT'S OVER BEFORE YOU KNOW IT

One year my birthday passed without time to celebrate. No cake, no party. I'd been working a lot. My daughter refused to believe I was a year older because I didn't blow out any candles.

"If you don't blow out your candles, you'll never be 49," she said. I figured that was a good thing.

I am still 49 as I write this, now and forever, just so you know.

I don't worry about age, though I spend too much money on a moisturizer by a company called Bliss. The moisturizer's called "The Youth As We Know It." I like companies with a sense of humor about laugh lines. I like companies named for happiness, even if the happiness they're selling is overpriced.

Still, in my last forties-year, I wondered about time, the way it passed without my realizing it, how much I've wasted by focusing on the wrong things or the wrong people or the wrong landscapes.

"It's over before you know it," my father used to say about living.

"Patience, jackass," my father said that about living, too.

Every year for my birthday, my mother would make my favorite cake—red devil's food with maple frosting. It's a difficult recipe, at least that's what she always said.

"Can't you pick something else?" she'd say and sigh.

"For Christ's sake, do not stomp in the kitchen," she'd say when the cake was in the oven. "This one's sensitive."

"We'll see if it comes out this year," she'd say every year, and every year it would come out just fine.

I'm not sure what the fuss was about, except the recipe came from my grandmother, who was notorious for leaving out ingredients so no one could duplicate her recipes, which meant no one could ever replace her.

When my grandmother was dying, the last thing she told me was a recipe for lasagna. It was a secret she refused to pass to her daughters, even though they begged for it for years. My mother and her sisters prided themselves on their cooking, but their lasagna, according to my grandmother, didn't measure up. It was always too runny, too flaccid, never the right balance of sauce and cheese.

It wasn't about lasagna, of course.

"They think they know everything. Smartasses," my grandmother said about her daughters. "I already forgot everything they don't know."

I don't know what was between my grandmother and her children. I don't know why my grandmother decided to pass a family recipe to me. It seems complicated, but it was probably something simple. Spite, maybe.

Growing up, I thought my grandmother loved me, but now I don't think she even liked me much. I was adopted, not her blood. My grandmother believed in blood. I was 19 years old when she died. I'd gone off to college to become a writer. My grandmother thought I was lazy because I read a lot. She told people I was a secretary, something useful like that. I wasn't much of a cook.

As for the recipe, she said, "Don't tell anybody."

The lung cancer that was killing her made it hard to talk, but she gasped out ingredients, directions, and dug her fingers into my skin so I'd pay attention. Her fingernails left marks, little parentheses on my wrist.

Spite is a strong motivator, I think.

"They'll screw it up," she said.

She said, "And then what?" and looked at me like so much depended on the answer.

She asked me to swear to keep her recipe secret and I swore, so I won't share it now, though it has something to do with nutmeg. I've followed the recipe and made it many times and it never comes out right, which makes me think my grandmother, in all her last-days' drama, punked me on her deathbed.

"I think it's about mortality," I said the other night to my friend, Ed, though we weren't talking about recipes. We were talking about writers, why some people wrote so many books.

"People shouldn't write so much," he said, but I disagree. I think writers should write as much as they can. Not because it makes them immortal, not because, as Ed would say, they'd be trying "to write for the ages," but because writing is work, maybe not in my grandmother's eyes but in mine. It's what writers are made to do. It gives us purpose.

It says, "I was here."

It says, "Maybe this life mattered a little."

It's useful in the way a recipe can be useful. It goes on feeding people. Or it leaves them hungry for that one small irretrievable thing that goes with us when we die.

I can't tell you about the lasagna, but here's my grandmother's recipe for that cake, which I know works because I've made it for my kids and everyone I love. The recipe is exactly as my mother typed it out on the typewriter she and my father gave me for my birthday when I was in 8th grade. I still have the typewriter, a grey portable Royal. It was the greatest gift I ever received because it meant my parents believed in me and what I wanted from life, whether they understood it or not.

RED DEVILS FOOD CAKE 1 ½ Receipt
    2-1/4 c. sugar (cream good
    3/c c. spry (add eggs
    3 eggs
    3 scant tbls. Cocoa + a little more
    3 c. flour —sift 3 times
    1-1/2 c. buttermilk
    1-1/2 teas. Soda
    1-1/2 teas. Vanilla
    1-1/2 tbl. White vinegar
    Pinch salt
    1-1/2 ounce red coloring
Pour in well greased pans. Bake at 350
for 30 to 35 min.

My mother typed recipe as Receipt, which is right, I think—recipe as proof of an exchange, a transaction between generations.

But it's the passed-down vagueness—cream good, plus a little more, sift 3 times—that bugs me. It sounds like mystery and magic, like something I'd learned in New Orleans when I visited the Voodoo Museum and put a wish in a tree stump. I wrote the wish on an index card, a recipe card. I used a tiny pencil stub.

I made two wishes, actually. They read:

    1) I wish my father a good death.

    2) I wish to be happy.

I put these wishes, with all their seriousness, into a fake plastic tree stump in a shop full of voodoo-doll key chains, sandwich-bagged potions, and dead snakes floating in jars of formaldehyde. It was all a joke, but it wasn't.

I was sad. My father was dying.

I wished him a good death although I knew there was no such thing. I wished for happiness, but I'd hung a quote by Colette above my writing workspace. "Who said you should be happy? Do your work."

This was a few months before I turned 35. I was floating in my own little jar.

I was home that year for my birthday. My father would die two weeks later, my mother five years after that. My father hadn't been eating much. Still, we were a family that believed in things, so my mother made the red devil's food cake.

"For Christ's sake, don't stomp," she said, but she sounded exhausted. My mother was a nurse. She'd been taking care of my father for a long time. I'd moved home to help with the end.

As for the cake, it came out fine. My mother lined it with candles.

"We'll count in fives," she said, and put seven candles on top. "We don't want to burn the house down."

My father got up from his rented hospital bed. He walked to the kitchen. He sat in his chair at the far end of the table. He asked for a piece of cake. A big piece.

"Delicious," he said, though he ate only a few bites.

This is my last memory of my father, fully conscious, his knit cap pulled low over his forehead, even so close to death embarrassed by what cancer had done to his hair.

"Here's to happiness, sweetheart," he said and raised his fork in a toast.

INCISIONS

The nurse who preps my mother for surgery is kind. She wears clogs and a smock with balloons and rainbows all over it. Her hair is pulled into a high ponytail. Overhead, the TV is tuned to *Good Morning, America.* The sky over America is popsicle blue.

"I like your uniform," my mother says, her voice thick, cottoned. "You know, I used to be a nurse."

"We make the worst patients," the nurse says. She undoes my mother's hospital robe. "You're not going to give me any trouble, are you?"

"Not me," my mother says, half smiling.

The nurse lifts my mother's right arm, then her breast out of the robe. The breast lolls to the side, soft and white against blue cotton, like a cloud but heavy and full of rain. The skin is stretched thin, and I can see the veins underneath. The areola is large and brown and I remember when I was young and first saw my mother naked, how astonishing it was, how I couldn't imagine ever being like her.

In the shower, her breasts would hang nearly to her waist. Later, when she'd get dressed, she'd have to bend over and lift them into huge pointy cups, first one breast then the other. She'd snap the bra closed, four hook-and-eye clasps, before she'd stand up.

"Be happy," my mother would say when I was a teenager, hopeless, flat-chested with Band-Aids taped into two flesh-colored x's instead of a bra. "Be grateful you'll never have to carry all this weight around."

Since then, I've bathed my mother. I've dressed her. I know her body the way I know my son's, the way I will know my daughter's, better than my own.

The nurse marks my mother's breast with a series of small x's. "To show the doctor where to cut," she explains.

The marks look like stops on a road map. They look like intersections. The nurse uses a purple marker. On the outside of the marker, there is a ruler and an ad from a pharmaceutical company called Allegiance.

"Here," the nurse says. She snaps the cap on the marker and hands it to me. "You might as well keep it. We can only use them once."

The drugs pull my mother in and out of consciousness. The sheets on the bed and the gurney are starched and white, the edges tucked into tight triangles, sturdy and sure.

I'm a child again, sitting on the edge of my mother's bed, watching her dress for work—her powdered legs, the sharp cut of her calves, her delicate ankles. "Still good," she says, "legs are the last thing to go," the white panty hose sheer as communion wafers, a few stray black hairs at the edge of her right knee where the razor always misses, the stiff nurse's cap, an origami swan she anchors to her dark curls, the picketed row of bobby pins, the square-toed shoes spotless with Sani-White.

"Now I feel more like myself," she says to me, to the mirror.

I'm a teenager, driving to Braddock Hospital over rutted brick roads, past boarded storefronts and shattered windows, past what used to be the flower shop, the donut shop.

"This used to be someplace," my mother says, illuminated in the passenger seat under streetlights, the pinhole of a camera, a white flash.

She is home, blood on her uniform. I don't know whose.

"There's only so much anyone can do," she says.

Before the nurse wheels her away, my mother leans her head to me. "Heart of my heart," she says, as she's always said to me, her adopted and only child.

I hold onto her hand before the doors to surgery snap open and I have to let go.

I put the purple marker in my purse.

"You should have been a nurse," my mother tells me when I help change her nightdress, when I bring her pills, when I lie next to her as she's dying. "You would have made a good nurse."

In lectures I talk about what I do — writing, the teaching of writing — as a useful thing.

I have never been able to heal anyone with words.

Later, I'll use the purple marker the nurse gave me to grade student essays. I'll write things in the margins, like "comma splice" and "cut." I'll write "Fragment" and "More."

I'll write, "Come closer."

I'll write, "What are you afraid to say?"

HOLY

My mother worries about my soul. She tells me so at her kitchen table, 6 a.m. We're making nut-roll, even though it's not a holiday, nothing to celebrate.

My mother believes bread rises only in the morning. I'm not good with mornings. Last night I stayed up late, writing, reading, worrying.

"Ruining your eyes," my mother says.

Drinking.

I'm hungover.

My mother is dying.

Everything is urgent now.

My mother wants me to know things, like where she keeps the silver, how to shut off the water, how to make a decent nut-roll.

"Who will teach you when I'm dead?" she says, and pounds the dough so hard it makes death seem impossible.

This morning she wants to talk religion, something I've refused to do for years. She brushes flour off her velour pantsuit. She punches the dough like it's a face, mine.

She says, "You can't believe in nothing."

She says, "If you don't believe in anything, what is there?"

She says, "You idiot."

I clutch the coffee she's made, instant, too much cream and sugar, the way my father liked it, not me. He's dead five years. I sit in his chair. The mug I'm holding was his, Batman, the image faded from my father's hands. My mother's mug, full of lemon tea, is Robin, faded to a mask and cape and the word "Holy!"

My mother would kiss my father's bald head.

She'd say, "The dynamic duo."

"First one goes, then the other," the funeral director said.

*   *   *

My dying mother wants to talk about god and faith over a pastry I'll never master no matter how important it is for her to hand this down.

A good daughter would say the words.

A good daughter would ease things.

"It's private," I say about my beliefs.

My mother says, "I changed your diapers and you talk about private."

She works the rolling pin like a threat. It was my grandmother's, then my mother's. Now it will come to me. The wood is worn to a honeyed shine, maple, like the trees my mother and I planted in the yard when I was a child.

My mother rolls the dough in a circle thin enough to see through, a lens to another dimension where she's still young, a Kool cigarette between her pink-tipped fingers, smoke rings rising from her lips, messages to decode.

The skin on my mother's hands is thin enough to see through, a lens to bone.

"I can't," I say about rolling dough that thin.

"Patience, jackass, patience," my mother says.

I'm trying.

*   *   *

"You'll go to hell," she says. "You know that."

On the table rests a blue prayer book, a tiny paperback my father carried in his pocket when he was sick, Daily Devotions, a Jesus fish in a circle on the cover. The fish is drawn in one line—no beginning, no end.

*   *   *

My mother doles out ground nuts and sugar, cinnamon and warm milk, four spoonfuls to make the sign of the cross. I spread the mixture evenly, as thin as the dough, thinner, out to the edges because it's expensive and has to last.

Once at a wedding, my mother brought nut-roll for the cookie table. Someone else brought nut-roll too, but it wasn't pretty, the layers and dough too thick.

"What asshole brings a nut-roll like that?" my mother said, then put her perfect nut-rolls on a tray. She carried them table to table to be sure people knew which ones were hers.

*   *   *

All my life, I've loved my mother.

All my life, I've disappointed her.

I'm not the daughter I want to be. I'm not the daughter my mother wants.

"You have to believe or you'll burn," my mother is saying.

The nut-roll spreads between us, a black hole, a universe pocked with stars.

*   *   *

Once I got stoned with a scientist who tried to explain Einstein's theory of time and space. He held up a

Taco Bell burrito he'd split in two. He showed me the layers. He said time was like that, a tortilla folded in on itself, now and not now, forever, amen.

"Time is not a clock and we are not second hands," he said, and swallowed the burrito down.

*   *   *

"It's all a horrible day-mare," Robin said to Batman.

*   *   *

It's been 13 years since my mother died.
She said, "You have to try to believe."
She said, "Do it for me."
She said, "Where will you be when I'm gone?"

Today a writer sends me a note that says she has a benefactress and the benefactress wants the writer to get a literary haircut. The writer has written to me for advice. She wants me to recommend a salon that specializes in literary haircuts.

These are the words the writer uses.

Benefactress.

Literary.

Haircut.

The benefactress will pay for the haircut. Cost is not a factor. The writer says the benefactress is worried about how the writer will look at upcoming literary events. The benefactress and the writer both want the writer to be taken seriously at literary events.

I don't know what the writer means by a literary haircut, or why she would write to me for advice. I'm not famous. I barely have any readers. My current hair makes me look like a human Q-Tip.

I believe this woman who's written to me has never seen my picture.

*　　*　　*

"Have the guts to cut," Kurt Vonnegut said, but of course he was talking about writing.

*　　*　　*

I don't know any benefactresses in 2017, but back in the 1990s I had some friends who gave me things. I was living in New York then, working for the airlines. I didn't have much furniture, and some of the things I did have were more like props. Since I was gone most of the time, I figured it might be good if the apartment looked lived in just in case some luckless burglar happened upon it.

I had a stereo that didn't work and a toaster that sparked and a TV that got only one channel because I couldn't afford cable. I had a few pots and pans and a window air conditioner that my neighbor Moose snagged from his Waste Management rounds.

Moose was part garbageman, part treasure hunter, and even though he once worked as a leg-breaker for the mob, he was big-hearted, always finding useful stuff in the trash he was paid to throw away.

He'd bring home gifts for me and our other neighbors, whatever he found that he thought we'd need. He brought home anything metal, too, and chopped it up with a chainsaw, then sold it at the junkyard for cash. "Everything's money to me," Moose said.

"It runs," he said about the air conditioner. "Just watch out for the mold."

I propped the air conditioner in a window for show. I set up the TV and stereo in my couchless living room. I used the pots Moose found to boil water on my tiny apartment stove which, whenever I lit it, smelled like it might explode. I had a drawer full of take-out menus. I had a refrigerator covered in magnets from take-out joints. I had a box under the sink full of wooden chopsticks, plastic forks, and spoons.

"A couch would make this place feel homey," a rich friend said, and measured a blank wall with her eyes.

I worked for the airlines for a reason. I didn't want homey. Life, I figured, was simpler without a couch to lug around. I considered myself a writer first, the kind of person who didn't care about a home and material things, the worry and weight of that.

I didn't consider that, without the weight of something like family and home, I didn't write much. I didn't consider that all the time spent alone in hotel rooms let me stay on the surface of things.

Stay on the surface too long and you get confused. You start thinking things matter that don't matter.

Literary haircuts, for instance.

* * *

"Pity the reader," Vonnegut said, which reminds me of how dangerous it is to put ego above art.

"Say what you mean," Vonnegut said, which means no tricks.

"I am what I am and that's a man from Indiana," Vonnegut would say about writers worrying over appearances on or off the page.

* * *

When the writer looking for the literary hairdo writes to me, it's her use of the word "benefactress" that pisses me off. It's that word that lets me forgive myself for being a jerk when I should be kind. It's not just about appearances. It's about class. It's about money, the lack of it, the elevation of it, how worry about money can make me mean.

I write back and say I got my last haircut at Supercuts.

I tell her it was $13 plus tip.

I tell her my benefactress, also known as my jug of quarters, thought that was cool.

I am thinking of taxes, the phone bill, the water bill. I am thinking of writing, how I want more time for it, how little it pays. I am thinking of the extra job I'll need to get this summer to help my family get by and how that extra job means I'll have less time for my family and writing, the things I love above all else.

I congratulate the writer on having a benefactress. I wish her and her hair well.

*   *   *

Later I will write about this on Facebook. I will consider tweeting. It's a shitty thing to do, but I can't help it. My anger at this woman, this stranger who means no harm, muddles things.

"Keep making that face," my mother used to say when I'd stick my lower lip out to show I was furious as a kid, "and a bird will come and shit on your lip."

"Keep making that face," my mother would say, "and you'll freeze like that."

That's the danger of class-anger, maybe. It can become something solid, immoveable, something that hardens inside a person and will not melt.

*   *   *

"I come from a working-class military family," the singer Pink says. "We watch the news and read the papers and vote, so there's always something to be upset about. I always have a certain amount of angst in my back pocket."

*   *   *

My poor writer friends and I post many pictures of terrible haircuts.

"Perhaps consider the Ken Burns," my friend Emily writes.

She posts a link to a story titled "Where's Your Precious God Now? 16 Intense Zooms of Ken Burns' Hair."

Ken Burns has a bowl cut. He looks like a demented Beatle. He looks like a toddler running with scissors cut his bangs.

*   *   *

"You have to curate your image," a rich writer I know says. "You have to work it."

Having a look takes time and money, neither of which I have. I have my family, two jobs, and a house with bad plumbing. These are the things I think about.

This particular writer spends a lot of time on Facebook and Twitter and Instagram. She's paid an advertising firm to turn her into a brand. She's paid a publicist to spread the news. She ran a contest where people had to send in pictures of her book in exotic places, kind of like Flat Stanley. People sent in pictures of her book at a café in the French Quarter, at a barbecue joint in Texas, at The Football Hall of Fame.

I forget what people won if they sent in pictures.

Another copy of her book, I think.

This writer has a sunken bathtub and no kids.

This writer has very nice hair.

*   *   *

"If you want to survive, you have to stand out," my friend Debbie used to say.

Debbie was a hairdresser at Vidal Sassoon in New York. Debbie wore all black, all the time, and had a huge tattoo of an eagle on her back. She also had her clit pierced and enjoyed talking about it over dinner with people she'd just met.

"I can squeeze my legs together any time I want and come, just like that," Debbie would say. She enjoyed watching people squirm as they struggled not to look under the table to see if Debbie was about to have an orgasm with her salad.

Debbie had gotten both the clit piercing and the eagle from a tattoo artist who worked with the New York chapter of the Hell's Angels. The tattoo guy hooked Debbie up with the Angels, who once let her do a hairstyle photo shoot in their clubhouse in the Village.

Debbie gave the Angels free haircare products in exchange for the photo shoot. The Angels, she said, liked haircare products. The Angels, Debbie said, thought a lot about their image.

"It's not like before," she said. "They have a guy who does their marketing and social media. They do charity work. They're very media-savvy."

*   *   *

I do not tell the writer who writes to me for hair advice that I cut my hair so short because I felt overwhelmed and old and *Prevention Magazine* said a pixie cut was just like a facelift and guaranteed to make a person look less tired.

"A boost for the spirits and cheekbones," *Prevention Magazine* said.

This has nothing to do with writing. It has to do with bills and work and bad plumbing, everything that's not about writing.

*   *   *

New York is filled with awful and beautiful people, Debbie would say.

Debbie used to do my hair for free. I'd be her hair model. We had a deal—she could do whatever she wanted and I wouldn't complain and I wouldn't ever have to pony up money.

A haircut at Vidal Sassoon in New York in the 1990s was well over $100. A blow-out was nearly that much.

I often bought groceries with my credit card and got cash advances to help cover my rent.

"Fake it until you make it," Debbie said as she globbed bleach on my hair.

"Everybody needs a gimmick," Debbie said as she took a razor to my bangs.

How Will I Use This in, Like, the Real World

I'm always happy to go back to school. It gives me an excuse to buy a new pair of shoes. I get giddy over office supplies—new pens, chunky notebooks, calendars filled with vacant to-do lists. I know. I'm old. My school shoes these days are sensible. But, as anyone in my family will tell you, I never really left school.

"You can't hide out forever," my aunts like to say. "Someday, you're going to have to get a real job."

I spent 20 years as a student. Now I'm a college professor. I'm a writer who teaches writing. I write too, of course, but I'm not Stephen King, which means I can't quit my day job. And most days, I wouldn't want to.

I choose to teach, am lucky to teach, although I have other, marketable skills. I'm an excellent typist. I've waited tables. I can work a bingo ball machine. And as a former flight attendant, I know both CPR and chokeholds.

But even though I choose to teach, I admit teaching writing is funny business. I teach what I love, which means it's personal.

"Can you tell me why I need to learn that? Can you tell me what that has to do with anything?"

This is my friend Cathy talking. Cathy hates writing as much as I hate math. The other day, she told me a story about her first college writing course. The instructor, a big redhead, wore elbow-length gloves, vintage dresses, and combat boots. She was supposed to teach comma rules, but one day she brought in a shoebox full of Barbie dolls and encouraged everyone to play.

"You'll note," she said, "there's no Ken. I never had a Ken doll. My Barbies were independent women. My Barbies had each other."

Her Barbies also had an elaborate wardrobe. While Ken was absent, his combat boots and flak jackets were not.

"Seriously," Cathy said. "What does that have to do with writing? What does it have to do with real life?"

I'd known Cathy's writing teacher. We'd gone to grad school together. We taught writing courses while we worked on our own writing and took seminars on how to teach. We were only a few years older than our students.

"Find new ways to stimulate thinking," our teaching-seminar professor said. "Make connections between the classroom and the world."

Cathy's instructor, a fiction writer, was into French postmodernism and feminist theory. She was probably well-intentioned and wanted her students to think about things like power and gender roles, but she didn't understand irony. Or maybe she thought irony was dead, a popular French theory at the time. Whatever her reasons, when she showed up in class with her stripped-down Barbies, she wore designer lipstick and face powder. She spent a lot of time and money in vintage stores and thrift shops, putting together a wardrobe that was half lunatic bride, half professional wrestler. These days, people would say she was curating her image. These days, she'd be a formidable presence on Facebook.

"I think we were all trying to sort it out back then," I told Cathy.

And it was true. It wasn't just Cathy's teacher. One day, a friend born in Cleveland would show up with a tweed blazer and a British accent. Another one would start collecting Elizabethan puppets and bring them to class whenever she had to talk about Shakespeare.

I took the Beat route. I wore black and sulked.

We were a mess — young writers trying to teach other young people why writing mattered, why anyone should care, and what use it and we, and maybe they, would be in the world.

"We tell ourselves stories in order to *live*," I'd say, quoting Joan Didion. I'd pause to make deep eye contact, like I could pull my students' souls like taffy, like I could mold them into the writers I knew they were born to be. They would look at me like my face was the moon. They would look at me like they were stuck at a stop sign with a cop behind them, like they were spelling out S-T-O-P.

"It would help," my mother used to say, "if you people weren't all so flakey."

I've been teaching for over 17 years now, and I'm slightly less flakey than I used to be, but I still haven't figured everything out.

A few years back, I gave what I thought was a fun assignment. I had my students write their own obituaries. This seems morbid, but at the time it felt practical. A lot of my students get jobs at newspapers, usually the obit desk. Not long ago, the obituary department of one of Pittsburgh's major daily newspapers consisted entirely of graduates from my university's writing program. It was something our Admissions people used in their pitches to prospective students.

"I don't get it," one student I gave the obit assignment to said. "How am I supposed to know how I'm going to die if I'm not dead yet?"

"Just make it up," I said. "Be creative. Throw yourself in front of a train. Get eaten by a shark. Go sledding on Everest. Make it up."

"I thought this was journalism," he said, and rolled his eyes. "We're not supposed to make things up."

"Whatever," another student, her eyes heavy with eyeliner, said. "It's all fake news anyway."

I wanted to tell her to stop watching Fox News. I wanted to tell her if there was one thing in the world that wasn't fake, it was death. I wanted to ask her what kind of eyeliner she used. But it was a morning class and too early in the day for all that and, besides, she'd grow out of it. We all do.

While my students worked on their obits, I did my own.

I'd drowned in a barrel of rare pinot noir while touring a Parisian winery. I was chased into the barrel by a pack of wild poodles. An investigation was ongoing. Prior to my tragic and untimely death, I'd been a world-famous writer and connoisseur of fine wines. I won the Pulitzer Prize. Twice.

"Are we really going to use this in, you know, like, the real world?" fake-news girl asked.

I wanted to tell her it didn't matter, that little we did would prepare her for what she called the real world and I called life.

"You'd be amazed," I said.

Back in college, the best and most practical class I ever took was Parapsychology 101. This was strange because I went to a Catholic college. I'm not sure how

Parapsychology 101 got past the priests who oversaw the curriculum. Exorcisms were covered in the course material, so maybe that cinched it, the Catholic Church holding the patent on exorcisms and all. Whatever it was, I'm grateful.

In Parapsychology class, we had guest speakers: a telekinetic who bent one student's house key with his mind, then forgot to bend it back; an ESP expert who used lines and squiggles to psychic-test the class; a medium who chatted with one student's dead grandfather until everyone was in tears.

Our professor, Dr. Z., had a collection of crystal balls and an Ouija board in his office. His favorite saying was, "Open your mind to possibility."

When I think about what makes teaching worthwhile—other than a paycheck and an ongoing excuse to buy new shoes—it's that. Possibility.

Every time I go into a classroom, there's the possibility that something amazing will happen, that, when my students and I leave, we'll have changed for the better.

"A creative writing class," Richard Hugo once said, "may be the only place you can go where your life still matters."

When I was growing up, I didn't know writers or artists. I didn't know anyone who would dress up in lace and combat boots and talk about Barbie's beauty myth. I didn't know people who read books, or anyone who would think that was important.

Most of the culture in Trafford happened at The Polish Club. The Polish Club had one of those bowling games where you sprinkle sawdust on the lane and knock the pins over with a hockey puck. It had a bar that was open seven days a week, bingo on Mondays and Wednesdays, and a fish-fry on Fridays. But weekends were what mattered most. That's when the polka bands would come in from Pittsburgh. People would get dressed up to hear them.

I started as a waitress at the club when I was 12, mostly in the bingo hall, but some nights, I'd work downstairs at the bar. The wood floor would shake from the music and the weight of people dancing. Everyone looked happy, and even the bartender, a notorious crank, would smack his hand on the bar and keep time.

Once, another man—because he was happy or drunk or because he took pity on me—tipped me $10 after I spilled his whiskey sour in his lap. I remember because I was 12 years old, and ten dollars was a lot of money, and it was illegal for me to be in a bar, and whiskey sours were what the women in my family drank at weddings and funerals. I remember because people usually tipped me a quarter. I was a kid and they figured I'd blow it on candy when what I really wanted was books.

"Don't worry about a thing, sweetheart," the man said as he shook ice cubes and cherries from his pant cuffs.

But worrying was what I did. It's what my parents did. The steel mills were shutting down. People were out of work. Every newspaper was writing our town's obituary. There wasn't much to do but sit around and think about bad luck. But when the doors of the Polish Hall opened and the bands kicked in, the music blocked that out. Men would overtip. Women in their high heels would pinwheel off the ground.

Now, at the beginning of every semester, I always ask a question.

"Why do you write?" I say.

I think this is a very smart question.

A few years back, one student, a girl decked out in day-glow orange, looked at me as if I'd been sculpted from belly lint.

"What do you mean by that?" she said.

"I mean," I said. "Why did you want to be a writing major? Why not engineering? Why disappoint your parents like this?"

"Math makes me break out in hives," she said. "Writing makes me happy."

So there.

I'd like to apologize here to my students for everything they've never learned. I'd like to tell Cathy that her instructor didn't mean any harm. I'd like to say one thing that, after all these years, I'm pretty sure of is that writing—the teaching and doing of it—might be flakey business, but it's important the way all art is important.

It makes us happy. It helps make sense of things. It allows us to be ourselves. It allows us to see what's possible. It gives us hope.

"The goal of all art," Camus said, "is to gain access to the one or two images that first gained access to our hearts."

A sawdusted bowling table.

A booze-soaked cherry rolling from a pant leg onto a wood floor.

A wood floor knicked and worn from dancing.

A ten-dollar bill a 12-year-old kid blew on books.

A polka band that came to town when people needed it most.

THE UNION PROJECT
*"Work is about a search for daily meaning
as well as daily bread."* —Studs Terkel

When my friend Syl asks me to work a catering gig, a hipster-ish wedding in a rehabbed church called The Union Project, I say, "I am so in," and she says, "Really?" like she expected me to say no.

It's been years since I've done restaurant work of any kind and I miss it. My first jobs were in kitchens and restaurants and, eventually, on airplanes, but I've spent the past 17 years writing books and teaching writing to college students.

It still feels awkward and embarrassing to say writer and college professor, though that is what I am, and most days, I love what I do. My students are sweet and earnest. Many of them are working-class, first-generation college students like I was. I could do without academic politics and academics that speak through their noses as if their giant brains squash their sinuses, but I know my luck.

I get time off to think and write. I get paid to teach what I love to students who often love it back. Some days, I feel like I smuggled myself in and stuck, like a wad of gum under my nice professorial desk.

I worry people will out me. Imposter syndrome, magazines call it, but it's not a real syndrome because many people have it.

Lots of us worry over our rightful place in the world.

*   *   *

"The pitcher cries for water to carry," the author Marge Piercy wrote, "and the person for work that is real."

The work I do is sedentary, head-based, abstract, and I sometimes worry about my own usefulness. I miss other kinds of jobs—concrete, physical work, the kind where, at the end of the day, you can see a measurable, tangible result.

Teaching and writing are useful in their own ways, of course—I believe this, I have to believe this—but they can feel weightless. It can take years to know if you're doing any good or not.

It's wonderful when my students who, by class and culture, would likely never publish books, publish books. Sometimes my name shows up in their acknowledgment pages. They send notes long after they graduate to catch me up on their lives. Sometimes they drop by my office to say hi. I get so excited, I weep at their success. By the time they are writers with books and chapbooks, though, I have lost them to their jobs and mine. The waiting period for success can feel a lot like failure.

This catering job is different.

"You're going to love her meatballs," Syl says about the caterer.

Syl says, "People go nuts for the meatballs."

The caterer's specialty is lamb-and-feta meatballs. Lamb-and-feta meatballs are neither abstract nor weightless. They are simple and delicious, unless you're vegetarian, in which case the caterer also makes a lovely and cruelty-free bruschetta.

Syl and I will serve said meatballs and bruschetta on silver trays to The Union Project wedding guests, who will dab their lips with cocktail napkins and take seconds and thirds, and Syl and I will smile and the guests will smile and everyone will go off happy into the night, amen.

"To be of use," Marge Piercy would call this kind of exchange.

*　　　*　　　*

Marge Piercy was born in Detroit to a working-class family. She was the first in her family to graduate college, and one of the first poets and writers I loved. Marge Piercy wrote about women I knew and recognized, though she lives in Wellfleet, Connecticut now. Wellfleet is known for its oysters and Noam Chomsky. It's the kind of place where summer is a verb.

But years ago, working-class Marge Piercy taught me that even though writing can feel frivolous, it's useful because it helps us stick around a while.

"Our work is to say: remember," Marge Piercy said. "Remember us. Remember me."

As long as people read, Marge Piercy said, everyone we love survives.

It's a romantic thought and one I pass to my students because I want it to be true.

*　　　*　　　*

Raised with physical work, I know enough not to romanticize it. Raised with physical work, I have a hard time seeing what I do for a living as real.

"It's only work if it shows in your hands," my grandmother Ethel used to say. Then she'd look at my hands — smooth, long-fingered, foreign — and frown.

*　　　*　　　*

LORI JAKIELA

"You don't know what work is," the poet Phil Levine wrote.

I think he was talking to himself and to me and to everyone like us, too—people who grew up one way and then, through luck or hard work or both, ended up somewhere else.

Like Marge Piercy, Phil Levine grew up in Detroit. He started working in car manufacturing plants at 14. His dad had owned a used auto parts business, but his mom was a bookseller and encouraged her son to write poems. He wrote poems about working people, about Detroit, about being an insider and an outsider to that world all at once.

Phil Levine went from working at Chevrolet and Cadillac to sneaking into the University of Iowa and studying with Robert Lowell and John Berryman. He went from earning a mail-order Masters degree to finishing his MFA at Iowa, the best writing program in the country. He ended up teaching at universities for the rest of his life—Stanford and NYU and Columbia and Princeton and Berkeley among them. He retired from The University of California at Fresno after 34 years.

All that time, he never stopped writing about work or workers. Some critics mocked him for that, even after he won the National Book Award, even after he was named Poet Laureate. They said his poems had too many working people in them. They said he worked hard at reminding everyone he'd been a peasant. That's the cost, maybe, of straddling worlds like that.

"Would you give me one reason why I should consider this poetry?" the critic Helen Vendler said about Levine's work.

Helen Vendler didn't like that his poems included things like lunch pails and salami sandwiches. Helen Vendler liked poems that were more Keats-ian. She called Phil Levine kitschy, another Rod McKuen. He called her elitist.

"Helen is deaf to poetry," Levine said.

About her reputation as poetry's preeminent critic, he said, "Even a blind pig gets a truffle once in a while."

*   *   *

My father, the millworker, used to say, "Don't be like me. Don't work with your hands."

The story goes, when my parents first visited me in the orphanage, my father took a look at one-year-old me and said, "This one's smart. I can see it in her eyes. She'll go to college. She'll meet a good man."

My parents adopted me shortly after that, and my father made his prediction come true. His hard work paid for my tuition. It paid my rent. It paid for books. Sometimes it paid my bar tab.

When my father was angry with me, he'd say, "Little Miss College," his worst insult.

He'd say, "I have more brains in my ass than you have in your head."

He'd say, "I'm a smart man. I don't need college to tell me that."

He'd say, "You think you're too good for this?" meaning the life he gave me, which wasn't the life I'd been born into, which wasn't my own life at all.

A picture of Phil Levine hangs in my living room.

A picture of my father hangs there, too.

They're the last things I see when I leave my house in the morning and the first things I see when I get home.

"Remember where you came from," my father would say, a threat, a prayer.

*   *   *

As an adopted person, remembering where I came from is difficult. I don't understand roots. I've always wanted to belong, but I pride myself in not belonging. Both desires are sincere. Both make me feel a little lost.

There is no English word for this. There is a German word — *fernweh*.

It means being homesick for a place you've never been.

Maybe *fernweh* is the word I need.

My adoption records say I have German roots.

*   *   *

I look forward to the catering gig for all the reasons I've mentioned, and a big one I haven't.

I need the money.

A catering job means cash in hand. It means tips in an envelope. Taxes are coming due and our bathtub leaks and my kids need new shoes and expect some kind of summer vacation, even if it's just an overnight at a waterpark. Lately I've been eyeballing our roof and begging it not to leak and our gutters to hold out one more year.

My professor job doesn't pay what my students think it pays. My students think I'm rich. They expect me to take them to dinner at the end of the semester. They expect pizzas.

Sometimes I buy them pizzas. They deserve pizzas. I buy doughnuts. I bake them bread and feed it to them in class. I buy my students books I think will change their lives and hope they'll read them. I put my love for them on credit cards.

"You must revise your life," I tell my students like the words are my own and not stolen from William Stafford.

I lie to my husband about how much I'm spending.

I lie to myself about how much I'm spending.

My husband says, "Stop buying your students' love," but I don't think that's what I'm doing.

I'm embarrassed not to make what my students think I make, as if my salary is a reflection of the kind of education they're getting. I'm embarrassed not to make what my students think I make, as if my salary is a reflection of my own failures.

Sometimes, when my students come asking for advice about graduate schools, they'll say, "I'm going to be a writer and an English professor, like you," and I say, "That's great. Let's look at back-up plans, too."

I tell them not to pay for graduate school. I tell them to be sure they get scholarships, assistantships. I tell them not to take out any more loans.

I don't talk much about how adjunct professor salaries are much worse than my own and how an adjunct could make more as a greeter at Walmart.

I don't tell them about my husband, who went to graduate school for writing like me and ended up in his 40s with three published novels, going back for another Masters in social work because there were no professor jobs for him. I don't say that my salary after 17 years as a college professor is just a little more than I would be making if I'd stayed in my previous job with the airlines.

Flight attendants have flight benefits, so they fly for free.

Flight attendants have nice layovers in hotels I can't afford anymore.

I'd have to calculate that.

There's a lot I don't tell my students because I believe in their talents and goals and dreams. I want them to have goals and dreams. I want their talents to grow and go on forever into the worlds of money and success.

I don't want to crush anything. I know how important it is not to crush anything.

Mostly I tell them to stay out of debt.

"Be practical," I say. "Just in case."

"Don't be like me," my father used to say.

*   *   *

In a recent interview with *The New Yorker*, author Sherman Alexie said, "I was angry that I could be thought of as being part of the 'liberal élite.' Even inside the literary world, I did not follow an élite path. I am a poor, public-school kid who got lucky. The only non-minimum-wage job I've ever had is writing. And writing is a minimum-wage job for most writers. I grew up in poverty and worked as a doughnut maker, pizza man, dishwasher, secretary, and janitor."

He said it was important for him not to forget that.

He said it was important to him that other people knew that.

*   *   *

It turns out the bride whose wedding I'll be working is a former student.

Stacy's not only a former student; she's one of my best former students. Years ago, she finished a novel as her senior project. What kind of student writes a novel as her senior project when she's only required to write 40 pages? A working-class student, a first-generation college graduate, someone who felt she had something to prove and proved it.

Stacy's novel was a good draft about a lovely and smart small-town girl who has a pregnancy scare that leads her to ditch her guitar-strumming slacker boyfriend and follow her dreams to become a famous novelist.

The novel showed promise, though Stacy didn't publish much after graduation.

"The world keeps getting in the way," she told me the first few times we ran into each other and I asked about her writing.

She blogged about bad first dates for a while, Tinder and that fish site and so on, then got distracted, then went back to school to get her teaching certification. After a while, when I saw her, I stopped asking about writing because it seemed to make her feel awful to answer.

Stacy used to babysit my kids when they were very young and I had to teach night classes. She taught my son about Dungeons and Dragons. She showed him notebooks full of worlds she'd created. She helped my daughter build Spongebob Legos. She sat through too many Baby Einstein videos to count.

She's a teacher herself, now, elementary school kids, and I'm sure she's wonderful and loved, though I know more about her from Facebook than from real life because we haven't seen each other in a while, because she has been replaced by other students, and I have been replaced by everything in her life.

"Is it going to be weird?" Syl wants to know when I mention that the bride is my former student. It didn't occur to me that it might be.

"No," I say.

I say, "It will be wonderful."

I say, "I mean, how amazing a coincidence is this?"

I say, "How is this even possible?"

*　　　*　　　*

I believe in the universe and serendipity.

I imagine how amazing this is. I imagine the surprise on my former student's face.

I imagine what it would be like to have your former writing professor dole you some meatballs.

I imagine asking my former student if she'd like more bruschetta.

I see myself all in black, my hair twisted back for sanitary reasons, my apron covered in frosting from slicing wedding cake, everything about me sticky and untouchable, but loveable, I hope.

I see myself in sensible shoes, bagging trash that sloshes into them. I smell like cold chicken marsala. I smell like grease and sweat.

I believe in the dignity of all work.

I believe in the dignity of hard work most of all.

I love hard work most of all.

And then I think, yep, it might be weird.

*　　　*　　　*

It's weird.

During set-up at the wedding, Syl tells the caterer that the bride is my former student, that I'm a professor and a writer.

The caterer, whose name is Jean, freezes into a smile.

"But I was a flight attendant for seven years," I say.

I say, "I've waited tables since I was 12."

I say, "You should see me pour coffee in turbulence," and make like the ground is shaking.

In the airlines, we never say turbulence. We say, "rough air." It's important to downplay things, but I've forgotten that.

Syl got me this gig because I'm her friend, because we're neighbors. We talk about money. We talk about bills. She vouched for me as a worker, as someone who needs money, who has bills.

Jean the caterer doesn't know me at all.

I can feel Jean looking me over, dubious. Professor, writer. It sounds bad, I know.

She's wondering, I think, why I'm here.

She's wondering if I know how to work.

She's wondering if I will work.

I feel my grandmother's eyes, examining. "It's only work if it shows in your hands."

Jean is wondering how much slack she'll have to pick up when I try to slither out.

Or maybe this is all me, my self-consciousness and ego, my need to justify my life.

"I know how to work," I want to say.

I want to say, "I was raised to work. Promise."

*   *   *

"Writing is hard work and bad for the health," E.B. White said, but writing and teaching are not the same as ditch-digging. They're not the same as restaurant work. They're not the same as my father's days in the mill.

Graphite dust is bad for your health.

Molten metal that melts skin and bone is bad for your health.

Hemingway said writing was like bleeding.

My father never wore a wedding ring because his work made that dangerous. Machines that catch on wedding rings and take fingers are bad for your health. Companies that don't pay disability are bad for your health.

"Do you even know what work is?" Phil Levine would say.

Jean looks at me like we're on a reality show and I'm the weakest link.

*   *   *

When I came back home after getting a graduate degree in poetry — courtesy of luck and graduate assistantships and other kindnesses — my cousin Jeff, that dick, said, "They give people degrees in that?"

He said, "They give people degrees in shit-shoveling too?"

*   *   *

To Jean, I say, "I'm excited. Thank you!"

I say, "What can I do first?"

Her smile unfreezes a little.

She points me to the set-up room, to a line of sternos waiting to be lit. She points to a stack of aluminum trays waiting to be filled. She points to a bin of salad waiting to be assembled.

She says, kindly, "Well, welcome aboard."

*   *   *

E.B. White never did restaurant work, but he knew a little about other things. Farming, for instance.

E.B. White wrote *Charlotte's Web*.

"We're born. We live a while. We die," Charlotte the Spider said, about the meaning of everything.

BOOKS BY BOTTOM DOG PRESS

HARMONY SERIES
Portrait of the Artist as a Bingo Worker, by Lori Jakiela,
216 pgs, $18
The Thick of Thin by Larry Smith, 238 pgs, $18
Cold Air Return by Patrick Lawrence O'Keeffe, 390 pgs, $20
Flesh and Stones: Field Notes from a Finite World by Jan
Shoemaker, 176 pgs, $18
Waiting to Begin: A Memoir by Patricia O'Donnell, 166 pgs.
$18
And Waking: Poems by Kevin Casey, 80 pgs, $16
Both Shoes Off: Poems by Jeanne Bryner, 112 pgs, $16
Abandoned Homeland: Poems by Jeff Gundy, 96 pgs. $16
Stolen Child: A Novel by Suzanne Kelly, 338 pgs. $18
The Canary : A Novel by Michael Loyd Gray, 196 pgs. $18
On the Flyleaf: Poems by Herbert Woodward Martin, 106 pgs.
$16
The Harmonist at Nightfall: Poems of Indiana by Shari Wagner,
$16
Painting Bridges: A Novel by Patricia Averbach, 234 pgs. $18
Ariadne & Other Poems by Ingrid Swanberg, 120 pgs. $16
The Search for the Reason Why: New and Selected Poems
by Tom Kryss, 192 pgs. $16
Kenneth Patchen: Rebel Poet in America
by Larry Smith, Revised 2nd Edition, 326 pgs. Cloth $28
Selected Correspondence of Kenneth Patchen,
Edited with introduction by Allen Frost, Paper $18/ Cloth $28
Awash with Roses: Collected Love Poems of Kenneth Patchen
Eds. Laura Smith and Larry Smith
With introduction by Larry Smith, 200 pgs. $16
Breathing the West: Great Basin Poems by Liane Ellison Norman,
$16
Maggot : A Novel by Robert Flanagan, 262 pgs. $18
American Poet: A Novel by Jeff Vande Zande, 200 pgs. $18
The Way-Back Room: Memoir of a Detroit Childhood
by Mary Minock, 216 pgs. $18

Acknowledgments Continued.

Thanks to everyone at the City of Asylum-Pittsburgh and Passa Porta Literary Center in Belgium for the incredible gifts of space and time. Thank you to my students, past and present, and everyone in the Pittsburgh writing community for reminding me what matters. Thanks most of all to Locklin and Phelan Newman. I love you more than anything in this world, and beyond that, and beyond that. And to Newman. For every good and true thing.

She meant temporary.

Some words Charlotte spun in her web: humble, radiant, terrific.

* * *

When Stacy makes her entrance, Jean says to me, "You should stand up front so the bride can see you."

Jean turns out to be a lovely person—a Buddhist in a t-shirt and black stretch pants, the most Zen of anyone who has ever done restaurant work ever, meaning she does not yell at people. She suggests.

Like, "Maybe you'd like to cut that bread."

Like, "The bride will want to see you."

Like, "Can you imagine how happy she'll be?"

Like, "Scootch forward a little."

I scootch. I make myself visible. I want to be visible and invisible. I feel like looking for a fire escape, a way out. I feel like blowing the bride a kiss.

I forget the song that's playing. I forget I'm in the way, blocking my co-workers who are trying to set up the bar, until George hits me with a hip to jolt me out of his way as he's filling a bin with ice.

Stacy, the bride in her lovely dress, moves toward where I'm standing. She looks left and right, smiling, a little shy but regal. Her hair is long and curled and she looks beautiful and grown, so grown, bathed in the rainbow light that pours through the stained glass windows above her. Instead of a veil, she wears a golden crown that weaves across her forehead like Grecian ivy.

* * *

Remember Keats' poem "Ode on a Grecian Urn," truth and beauty, beauty and truth?

Critics hated that poem, the way it was based on an ordinary object, a vase of all things, and Keats died thinking it was terrible and inconsequential, and then years later Helen Vendler, who hated the salami and lunch pails in Phil Levine's poems, would love Keats' urn so much she'd build her reputation on it.

It's hard, maybe, to see the meaning and value of things in real time.

*   *   *

When Stacy finally sees me, I give a little wave. She looks confused. Then shocked. Then embarrassed. Then happy.

Then shocked and happy and embarrassed and confused, all those emotions circling each other, figures on a vase that never connect.

*   *   *

I go back to the kitchen. I load up a tray with meatballs. I raise the tray above my head, the way I've known how to for years.

I am proud of my muscle memory. I am proud of my balance and skill.

I put on a smile.

It's a good smile, practiced but sincere.

It says, "Welcome."

It says, "I'm here to serve."

*   *   *

When I teach, I always bring my students a little something. A candy bowl. Some brownies or cookies I've made. The bread I mentioned.

Did you know Oreos are vegan?

Twizzlers and Skittles are, too.

My students have needs that are bigger than I can imagine.

I have needs that are bigger than they can imagine.

"After a good meal, you can forgive anyone," Oscar Wilde said.

I give my students' food not to buy their love, but because I need their forgiveness — for failing them; for the inevitability that the world will be too much; for the fact that I know this and encourage them to be writers despite it.

I want to invite my students into my life and hold them there.

I am afraid of the weight of this, so we stick to snacks.

I know I will fail everyone and be sorry for it.

Here's something small and sweet.

Maybe you'll write about this someday.

Maybe you'll remember me for this.

*   *   *

Sometimes Syl and I talk about opening a business together in Trafford, our hometown. We would love to own a little café. Trafford could use some good coffee. Trafford could use a place where people could come and sit a while. Syl makes beautiful cookies and pastries. I know some things about coffee.

Trafford recently built a new police station and put the old one up for sale. Syl and I dream about buying it. We'd turn it into a cafe called The Clink. Our logo would be a coffee cup run along prison bars. We'd have coupons that would look like speeding tickets and our décor would be black-and-white stripes. We'd go full on with the incarceration theme. Our espresso would be called Mug Shots and our slogan would be, "Coffee so good,

you'll be here for life." We'd have a house band that would do covers of "Folsom Prison Blues" and "I Fought the Law" and "Bang Bang (I Shot My Baby Down)."

"We could really do this," Syl says, and we both imagine it.

Imagining is lovely, but money is another thing.

We drive by the station again and again. We park and walk around the building. We hold up our hands like picture frames. Inside the old police station, there are holding cells. Syl and I figure we would leave them as is. Business people could reserve the cells the way they reserve private meeting rooms at Panera.

We would book The Clink's cells by the hour. If people want, we could lock them inside.

It would be something people would pay extra for, to be trapped like that.

*   *   *

"Most of us have jobs that are too small for our dreams," Studs Terkel said.

Here's the thing about dreams — they can make a person disgruntled. Dreaming is a costly pastime.

Syl checked out how much we'd need to buy The Clink. "Just around 20," she says, meaning $20,000.

Dream too much and the world can seem sadder and more ridiculous than it is. Dream too much and you can give up on the small good things the world can offer.

"Be satisfied," my father said, his key to happiness.

I never knew my father to be happy.

$20,000 might as well be Mars. It might as well be the head of Walt Disney reanimated from whatever freezer it's frozen in. It might as well be the reanimated head of Walt Disney channeling Porky Pig.

That's all, folks.

*   *   *

At Stacy's wedding, I pass meatballs. I pass bruschetta. Everything is delicious and beautiful and anything but simple. My feet hurt like they do not when I sit behind my desk. My back hurts and there's a twinge in my neck that's different from the twinge I get when I'm at my computer too long.

The more I serve, the more I realize. There are other former students here, lots of them. One thing about my students — they tend to stay friends. It's something I brag about, our community of writers.

Stacy has invited a dozen or so of the people who graduated with her. One of them, I remember, pulled a pocketknife in a writing workshop once because people didn't like the poems he'd been writing. His poems had a lot of dead deer and aliens in them. One former student, her dress studded with sequins, never turned her work in on time, but her work was always good, full of anger and grit, anti-sequins. Each of my former students looks more shocked and, maybe, horrified when I lean over and offer appetizers.

"Oh my god," one says.

"Jakiela?" one says.

"What are you doing here?" another one, TJ, says, like he just caught me dumpster diving, and I say, "What, this?" I say, "I love this kind of work." I say, "This is the first time I've done it in a while." I say, "The money's good." When I laugh, it sounds forced.

*   *   *

I could ask TJ why he's here, too.

TJ was Stacy's boyfriend for years, and now he's a guest at her wedding to someone else.

It seems awkward at best.

Instead I say, "Look at you!" and step back to take him in. I balance my tray of meatballs on one hand and reach down to attempt a hug. TJ is thin and pale as ever, his arms and legs jutting like pipe cleaners beneath his black suit.

Back when TJ was my student, over 10 years ago, he was artsy, an activist, always working for this or that cause. He worked with Stacy on the school literary magazine. He took photos and wrote a little, too, though his double-major in philosophy didn't help his writing much. His poems were abstract, full of deep thoughts, no people or salami in them. Still he was smart and sweet and earnest, bent on changing the world. I liked him very much.

TJ wore black all the time, but by black I mean band t-shirts and jeans, never a suit. TJ wore his dyed black hair in dreads and had his eyebrows pierced. Today TJ's eyebrows are clear of studs, but his hair is still dyed black, still in dreads, though the dreads look somehow coiffed. When he hugs me, I feel something heavy on his wrists—gold cufflinks.

I bring the tray of meatballs down between us and offer him some, then I remember he was a vegetarian and probably still is.

I say, "Sorry," and he says, "No worries."

Two boys are with him, one on each side. They're around my daughter's age, 10 and 12, maybe. The boys snag the meatballs TJ passed on. They take seconds and thirds. The boys are handsome, with long wavy rich-kid hair. They're both in suits with bow ties. The suits look expensive. The bow ties are hand-tied, not cheats.

TJ introduces them as his stepsons. It takes me a minute to let that register.

TJ, who always had trouble growing facial hair, still seems to have trouble with facial hair. He has a scraggy goatee. His sideburns are spotty. That he is a father to two boys who look like they summer in the Hamptons feels impossible. But those cufflinks are impossible, too.

He says, "Life's crazy, right?"

He says, "Oh, this is my wife, Carol."

I hadn't noticed Carol until now, maybe because she's been ignoring our exchange. Her body is turned at an angle, away from TJ and her sons. She looks much older, rich. She looks like the least-likely person to be married to TJ ever. She has expensive blonde hair, highlights in every buttery shade of gold. Her dress looks like something Coco Chanel would like. She is wearing a brooch.

TJ tries twice to introduce us, but Carol will not look at me. TJ seems embarrassed by this, so I try to cover for him. I offer the wife a meatball. I give her a smile. She puts up her left hand to wave me off.

The diamond she's wearing is huge.

*   *   *

When I was a flight attendant, there were stories of celebrities who sent their assistants to board the plane first. Oprah. Steve Martin. Lucille Ball. Lucille Ball died before I started flying, but her reputation was legendary.

"Ms. Ball does not speak to the hired help," her assistant would say.

"Do not look Ms. Ball in the eye," her assistant would say.

"Direct any questions for Ms. Ball to me," her assistant would say.

Now, TJ's wife looks like I'm taking in too much air. I'm making it hard for her to breathe.

I say excuse me. I say I have to get back to work.

TJ says, "We'll catch up later." He says, "It's good to see you, even so," and shrugs.

Later, when I come to pick up trash, TJ's stepsons and Carol the wife will pretend I'm invisible.

*   *   *

I feel bad that my former students seem embarrassed that I'm serving them, but I don't consider what it means until later. The work is non-stop—plating salads, serving, clearing, main course, cake. An older man is angry because he wants more meatballs. I bring him more meatballs. Syl and I make plans to go out for drinks when our night's over to celebrate. I love the way my body feels—tired, in motion. I love how it makes it hard to analyze anything too much.

*   *   *

When I think about serving my students, I realize it's always been like this between us.

Here's a meatball. Here's bruschetta.

Here's a book of poems. Here's a book of stories.

Have you written something beautiful and true? Send it to me.

*   *   *

At the end of the night, the bride and groom are very drunk. They are beautiful and young and emotional. The groom comes back to the kitchen twice to tip us, again and again. I hug the bride and pretend I have not been twice-tipped. She tells me she wants to

get back to her novel. We make plans to get together to talk about that soon, though I know we probably won't.

All my co-workers count out their cash on the steel prep table.

They are happy about the extra tips.

I am, too.

ABOUT THE AUTHOR

Lori Jakiela is the adopted only child of a millwright and a nurse who both believed work was work only if it showed in your hands.

"You don't know what work is," Jakiela's father said about his daughter's smooth hands. It was one of his worst insults.

It's also a line from a poem by Philip Levine.

"How long has it been since you told him / you loved him, held his wide shoulders, / ... and said those words," Levine wrote in "What Work Is."

Jakiela's father has been dead many years. Her mother too, though Jakiela goes on writing them the way writers do when they don't say everything that needed saying in this life.

About work: Jakiela knows some things about it now.

She's been a bingo worker, a waitress, a journalist, a bartender, a sportswriter who knows next to nothing about sports, a secretary, a Things Remembered key maker, a flight attendant, more.

Once, when she lived in New York City, she was almost hired as a porn writer but couldn't stop inventing story lines where her characters were interested in things other than sex, like grilled cheese and bath gel and episodes of "Friends" where the friends didn't work but could still afford New York rent. Impossible.

Jakiela left New York in 2000. Now she teaches writing at a university. She lives with her husband, the

author Dave Newman, and their two children in the house she grew up in, in Trafford, Pennsylvania.

Trafford was a mill town founded by George Westinghouse and named for Trafford, England. When she worked as a flight attendant, Jakiela visited Trafford, England. She rode the city bus and toured two castles and a bug museum. Many hard-working people there seemed obsessed with flesh-eating beetles, mummification and The Wu Tang Clan. Jakiela's still trying to figure out what this means.

The author of three previous memoirs and a poetry collection, she writes to figure things out, to connect the dots between all that beautiful strangeness.

"I like that the world is weird and I'm weird too," Jakiela's 12-year-old daughter Phelan likes to say.

Yes.

That.

For more, visit http://lorijakiela.net.